THE CHANGING ENVIRONMENT OF
INTERNATIONAL RELATIONS

THE BROOKINGS INSTITUTION

The Brookings Institution is an independent organization engaged in research and education in the social sciences. Its principal purposes are to aid in the development of sound public policies and to provide advanced training for students in the social sciences.

The Institution was founded December 8, 1927 as a consolidation of three antecedent organizations: the Institute for Government Research, 1916; the Institute of Economics, 1922; and the Robert Brookings Graduate School of Economics and Government, 1924.

The general administration of the Institution is the responsibility of a self-perpetuating Board of Trustees. In addition to this general responsibility, the By-Laws provide that, "It is the function of the Trustees to make possible the conduct of scientific research and publication, under the most favorable conditions, and to safeguard the independence of the research staff in the pursuit of their studies and in the publication of the results of such studies. It is not a part of their function to determine, control, or influence the conduct of particular investigations or the conclusions reached." The immediate direction of the policies, program, and staff of the Institution is vested in the President, who is assisted by an advisory council, chosen from the professional staff of the Institution.

In publishing a study, the Institution presents it as a competent treatment of a subject worthy of public consideration. The interpretations and conclusions in such publications are those of the author or authors and do not necessarily reflect the views of other members of the Brookings staff or of the administrative officers of the Institution.

THE CHANGING ENVIRONMENT
of
INTERNATIONAL RELATIONS

Brookings Lectures, 1956

GRAYSON KIRK   EDWARD S. MASON
HARRISON S. BROWN   HAROLD H. FISHER
DENIS W. BROGAN   WILLARD L. THORP

THE BROOKINGS INSTITUTION
Washington, D.C.
1956

© 1956 BY

THE BROOKINGS INSTITUTION

Set up and printed
Published July 1956

Library of Congress Catalogue Card Number 56-10954

37577   *Printed in the United States of America*
George Banta Company, Inc.
Menasha, Wisconsin

Foreword

THIS VOLUME presents the third series of Brookings Lectures, which were inaugurated in 1954 to encourage research in the social sciences. The first series, given two years ago, dealt with the relationship between economics and public policy and was published under the title of *Economics and Public Policy*. The second series, given last year, considered recent research developments in politics and government and was published under the title of *Research Frontiers in Politics and Government*. The third series, given earlier this year, was devoted to the changing environment of international relations, another field of interest in Brookings research and currently a major problem of United States foreign policy.

During and since the Second World War, American leadership and the American people have been striving to adapt themselves to the pre-eminent role in world affairs that events have thrust on the United States. The over-riding question has been whether conditions of lasting peace, based on security and justice, can be established in a world that consists of a large number of nation-states, each functioning on the basis of its own concept of its national interests. Wartime planning—more particularly American planning—for the postwar era took the approach that such conditions could be established if the nations would recognize and accept the existence of a common national interest, which it was assumed all of them had, in the preservation of world peace. Acceptance of such a common national interest had to be followed, however, by the creation of a framework of international relations within which differences and disputes between nations could be settled without recourse to the use of force. This required, in turn, acceptance by all nations—or at the very least by the major powers—of a minimum code of international behavior.

The validity of this approach, which guided the arrangements for making the peace treaties, establishing the United Nations system, and taking the other necessary steps along the road to creating a peaceful and secure world order, was soon questioned, however, in the light of postwar events. Conflict instead of accommodation, conflict that contained the very seeds of violence, came to prevail in relations between the Soviet Union and the free world, and at the same time, tensions began to develop among the nations and the peoples of the free world. In fact, it seemed possible that in the long run, the chances of preserving peace might depend more on whether the free nations could draw closer together and create the kind of world they would want when the Soviet-Communist threat would be ended, than on whether they could currently change the attitude of the Soviet Union and thus diminish the threat.

American leadership and the American people, therefore, have had to adjust to a new role in world affairs at a time when disillusionment and tension were rapidly growing, and when there was an increasing premium on wise American policy decisions. It was in these circumstances that the late Dr. Leo Pasvolsky—who until his death in May 1953 was Director of the International Studies Group at the Institution—began developing a program of proposed research designed to reappraise the earlier American approach to the problem of creating a basic framework for present day international relations. The program, which was not completed when Dr. Pasvolsky died, contemplated a comprehensive analysis of the principal factors that are conditioning and determining the conduct of nations in their current foreign relations.

Further study of the problem by the Brookings staff and consultants emphasized that the actual framework of international relations now is being profoundly altered by the dynamic forces that have been released by man's new knowledge of himself and of his natural environment and by the effects of this knowledge on his material, moral, and ethical values and on his institutions. Most of these forces would be in existence even if the cold war did not exist. Consequently, any substantial success in efforts to lessen tensions between the Soviet-Communist bloc and the free nations would bring into sharper focus the features of the changing world environment in which the American people must live.

The purpose of the third series of Brookings Lectures is to identify and briefly analyze the possible ways in which these forces might operate over the near future and, hence, the possible form in which problems of United States foreign policy might emerge during the next ten or twenty years. Fundamental changes, among the most important of which is the emergence of aspiring new nations in Asia and Africa and the disintegration of empire and colonialism, are occurring as a result of these forces. Such changes require a reexamination of many of the traditional and recent assumptions underlying relations between nations and will make necessary a further readjustment of United States relations with the rest of the world.

The series comprises six integrated lectures. The first two deal with the impact on international relations of man's increasing awareness of himself as a political, social, and moral being, and of his knowledge of his physical environment and his new skills and techniques in industry, agriculture, and health. The third lecture relates the broad area of the first two to the narrower focus of the conflicts among governmental and political institutions, based on differing ideas, values, and sanctions, through which man seeks to attain his domestic and international goals. The fourth lecture considers the new conditions created in international trade and financial relations by the efforts of governments to respond to the expectations of their peoples with respect to full employment and economic development. The first four lectures provide the broad framework for the last two in the series. These deal with the problems and prospects for co-operation between the newly emerged nations of Asia and the Western world, and bring the whole series to its climax.

These six lectures were given at approximately two-week intervals from early March to early May 1956. They were a feature of the celebration of the fortieth anniversary of the founding of the Brookings Institution, and the first lecture was given at the dinner held on March 10, 1956 that celebrated the anniversary. The plan for the series was developed by Maynard Barnes, under the general supervision of Robert W. Hartley, Director of International Studies.

The Institution is grateful to the Rockefeller Foundation for its financial support of the program of research in international relations out of which developed the background of the thinking and planning that led to this third lecture series.

ROBERT D. CALKINS
President

May 16, 1956

Contents

1

Mass Aspirations and International Relations

GRAYSON KIRK[1]

AN ANALYSIS of mass aspirations and international relations is not merely a matter of interest to scholars. It bears
directly on the making of foreign policy in this country—
and in others—at the present time. The first principle of wise
policy-making in foreign affairs is that the end product ought
to represent a judgment on the proper evaluation of two
forces. One of these is vision—which is what one would like
to accomplish if all obstacles were removed and one could
operate under ideal circumstances. The other is a realistic estimate of the road-blocks that are certain to prevent one from
reaching any ideal objective. A statesman can make such a
calculation only if he has the capacity for dispassionate and
searching analysis, a ready familiarity with historical evidence, and an almost intuitive ability to identify and to estimate trends.

This last quality is the true measure of statecraft. No one
can be certain that he can look into the seeds of time and
predict which will grow and what will be produced. But the
statesman must make the effort because the penalty for failure
to try may be as great as the penalty for wrong guessing. The
statesman who is oblivious to changing circumstances is as
much of a danger to his country as the man who is unable
to resist the temptation to tell his people what he thinks
will please them.

---

[1] President, Columbia University.

Changing Framework of Foreign Policy

Today is a peculiarly difficult time in which to estimate the changing trends that affect foreign policy. There are times in history when the current of affairs moves, as it were, slowly and sluggishly across an open plain. There are other times when the stream seems to be fed by rushing and unexplored tributaries and when its course is quickly hidden from view. Today, we struggle with a situation of unprecedented complexity, and yet we know that we dare not pay the penalty of drift because then we would really be—if I may use the word —at the brink.

If we undertake to compare our situation today with that of even the fairly recent past, we are impressed immediately by the change in what we might call the geographic framework of foreign policy. Until perhaps the time of the First World War, our Secretaries of State could virtually ignore developments in a large part of the world. They were required to maintain a close watch over Western Europe, and they kept a wary eye on happenings in this hemisphere. Elsewhere, the imperial domination of Western Europe and the lack of any important national interests of our own combined to reduce our concerns to the bare minimum of servicing the needs of international commerce and protecting the rights under international law of American citizens.

Our national interests are now bounded by the round world itself. Names and places, once remote and exotic, are now commonplace. Is there any place in the world of today in which political, social, and economic trends may not have some bearing on our own national welfare? Even the wastelands of Antarctica and the strategic importance of the stratosphere command our attention.

A century and a half ago one of the most respected of our Columbia professors spoke at a meeting of the New York

Historical Society and he offered a toast "To the Speedy Termination of our Foreign Relations." Today some of his spiritual descendants still exist, though I doubt if any of them are at Columbia, and they are sometimes elected to Congress, but they are a vanishing race. We now know, all of us, that what is done in Washington affects every part of the world, and we know that the relationship is reciprocal.

But the problem of the new foreign policy is not merely one of geographic dimensions. It applies also to the substance and the instruments of policy. With respect to each country, the range of our policy concerns is vastly greater than in the past. The tendencies of the press, the trends in the educational system, the formation of new political parties, the discovery of raw materials, industrial development, popular attitudes toward other countries—all these matters enter into the content of policy and must be weighed. Even more pronounced is the new impact of our own domestic pressures on the determination of policy. About this, I need not comment in the city of Washington.

As policy concerns have multiplied, so have the instruments. All of our government departments, and many of the independent agencies, have direct interests in foreign affairs, and they seek a hand in policy. Trade policy, financial policy, agricultural policy, mass propaganda policy—all are instruments that somehow must be co-ordinated lest they work at cross purposes. At times we speak abroad with so many voices that we can only hope that our opponents are as confused as we are regarding which is the authentic and official Voice of America. Victory in diplomacy is not likely to come to the negotiator who shares his innermost thoughts and plans with everyone before he sits down with his friends and his adversaries.

This is not a requirement of democracy; it is an invitation to disaster.

Emergence of Mass Attitudes

I have been asked in this lecture to draw your attention particularly to a third foreign policy consideration of growing significance throughout the world. This is the emergence of mass attitudes as an important factor in international affairs. In some respects it is one of the most striking phenomena of our time. In the earliest days of the state system, foreign affairs were the exclusive prerogative of the sovereign, and an ambassador was no more than his personal agent. As absolutism retreated, rulers accepted the obligation to consult with representatives of the people before reaching major policy decisions. Even so, the masses generally accepted the view that foreign relations should be managed by experts who brought to their task education, training, and experience. The people did not demand the right to participate directly in policy making.

Throughout large parts of the world today, this situation no longer obtains. Governments are now confronted with a demand for the widest possible popular consultation before policy is made. No official of a government is offered half as much advice, and by as many citizens, as the Foreign Minister. In this respect, his position is rather like that of a university president. The reasons for this are obvious. The first is literacy, or, rather literacy and communications. Hundreds of millions of people now know more about the outside world than their fathers did. Their knowledge may be less than full or accurate, but there is more of it. Through motion pictures, the radio, books, cheap magazines, and even television the world has been brought into their homes; vicariously at least, distant lands are no longer so distant.

The second reason is a new awareness of the relationship of the outside world to the individual. People know that their taxes are high because of the need to pay for past wars and current defense programs. They know that no matter where they live, they are exposed to the dangers of mass destruction launched from distant bases. They know that even if they are spared the rigors of war, their welfare is affected increasingly by the flow of international trade and investment.

In these circumstances, it is not surprising that the people have begun to demand with a new insistence that they have some direct voice in the shaping of policies. Spurred on by all the pundits of press, radio, and television, the people hold over the heads of their foreign ministers the constant threat of massive retaliation for mistakes or blunders. They know that their well-being, and even their lives, may be at stake.

It would be wrong to conclude that this transformation has taken place only in the more advanced democratic societies. Outside the Iron Curtain it is in varying degrees a universal phenomenon. The virtual liquidation of colonialism has given to uncounted millions of persons a new sense of civic participation and responsibility. These people may be illiterate, but they vote, and their attitudes and aspirations can no longer be ignored with impunity by their leaders.

Perhaps the most significant consequence of the great colonial revolution of our times is this changing attitude of the masses. The level of their expectations has been raised, and it moves constantly higher. Being free politically, they are now determined to gain, and to gain quickly, a substantial improvement in material well-being. Because of increased mobility and modern communications, men of the present generation know, as their ancestors never did, how badly off they are, in terms of standards of living, by comparison with many other peoples of the earth. One has the impression, in meeting their leaders and administrators, of great vitality, great devotion and great industry. They are determined to move their peoples quickly into the modern world. It is an inspiring experience to talk with them and to sense their drive and their dedication as they grapple with problems of staggering magnitude. These peoples, as well as their leaders, have a sense of being on the march. They have a grim determination to build a welfare state, and they will reject leaders who fail to move them forward quickly into the new era. They are far less concerned about ideological labels than about human welfare. They have mass determinations as well as mass aspirations.

This changing position of the masses of people in Asia and Africa has created a new dimension, and a new set of problems, for the foreign policies of the Western states. The change has come about quickly and dramatically. If there is a thesis in my remarks, it is that many of our present perplexities in foreign affairs stem from our failure to re-examine our foreign policy in order to make it more in tune with the mass aspirations of the non-Western world.

All nations must cope with the geographical expansion of their interests and with the multitude of new forces that affect foreign relations. In this respect the problem is much the same in Washington as in Moscow. But if we are becoming alarmed about the retreat of Western influences in Asia and the sturdy growth of Soviet encroachment, we could do worse than to seek an explanation in terms of the degree to which Soviet and Western policies respectively may be in tune with these aspirations of the Asian peoples.

You may believe, of course, that Western influence in Asia is wholly satisfactory. You may believe—and some people do —that we are successfully frustrating the designs of Soviet imperialism. You may believe that time is certain to be on our side. You may believe these and any other fairy stories that commend themselves to your imagination. But I have not come here to entertain you. I have come to talk about the world as I believe it is and not the world as I would like it to be. And the facts are both grim and disturbing.

Western Relations with Asia

With your permission I should like to devote a little time to this problem of Western relations with Asia. If we probe into it, we shall realize that it throws much light on the central problem of mass aspirations and international relations, which we are asked to consider in this lecture. It illustrates the new dimensions that foreign policy must have if it is to be successful. Equally, it points out the unwisdom of relying overly much on traditional attitudes and techniques. It is not a comforting exploration, but it is useful.

Today the heavy hand of the past hangs over Western relations with most of the peoples of Southern Asia, the Middle East, and many portions of Africa. Psychologically speaking, the evils of colonialism have lived after it, and much of its good has been interred with its bones. In dealing with these newly independent peoples, the men of the West have not yet cast aside their traditional and ingrained attitudes of superiority and paternalism. For too long the leaders of the West have had contempt for the East because of its lack of technical progress, its differing religious beliefs, and the squalid poverty of its masses. All too frequently, even the ablest colonial administrators have failed because they could not rid themselves of the corroding assumptions of racial, technical, and national superiority.

The Eastern peoples also bring into the modern world an unhappy legacy from the past. The spiritual refuge that they once found by denouncing the so-called "materialism" of the West now is no longer needed, but it will not be discarded for a long time to come. In their struggles for political emancipation, Eastern leaders found comfort and justification in forgetting the welfare features of colonial rule and in stressing policies of economic exploitation and social discrimination. So rigidly conditioned is this attitude that current Western policies and practices, such as technical assistance, can be denounced—to the tune of widespread popular approval—by Communists who charge that these are merely new manifestations of Western exploitation thinly disguised by Western hypocrisy.

The influence of this heritage of the past is sharpened by that abnormal sensitivity and belligerent assertiveness common to all newly independent peoples. If Americans become overly impatient with these attitudes—and we are an impatient people—we should do well to recall the history of American attitudes toward Europe a hundred and fifty years ago. To do so ought to give us more understanding of characteristics that are deeply rooted in all human nature.

These comments are pointed to the rather obvious conclusion that the normal nation-to-nation, give-and-take relationships that exist today between countries such as the United States and Great Britain will be difficult to develop in Western relations with the new Asian powers. Many Asian leaders have a far better understanding of the West than Western leaders have of Asia. But the legacy of the past weighs on East and West alike, and only time, expedited by intelligence, can improve the climate for our political relations.

Policy of the Soviet Union

It is this situation that the Soviet Union has undertaken to exploit for its own advantage. During their recent trip to India and Burma, the Soviet leaders repeatedly attempted to identify all the Western powers, including the United States, with colonialism and exploitation. The West was portrayed as being interested only in profits and callously indifferent to human suffering and mass aspirations for improved welfare. Comrade Khrushchev told the press, while in the Burmese Shan states:

. . . In the past the peasants were bred to be impressed into service and were told that only people chosen by God could rule. Simple peasants could not rise to any such position. But now in our state any man or woman, provided he has received a certain education, can participate in the Government. . . . I am going to say that the English were sitting here on your necks and were robbing your people, and . . . it was done not for your benefit or raising your standard of living, but in order to bring their civilization into backward countries. . . . But we say differently. They were sitting in these countries to rob the last piece of bread from the people. . . . We Soviet people are glad you have thrown off colonial oppression. We are ready to do anything in our power to help you so that there is no return of colonialism. We could be working for you, creating new lives for yourselves and your children, to be free and to possess new industries. This is our ambition. . . . You are living by your own labor and so are we. We can help each other. You help us and we will help you.[2]

To the peoples of Southern Asia, the Soviet Union thus identifies itself as the benevolent leader of the Asian peoples against the West. Carefully omitting reference to any distinctions between socialism and communism, the Soviet leaders place themselves in the position of the "Big Brother" who has emancipated himself earlier from capitalist exploitation, who has grown to great strength under the new and beneficent system, and who seeks to help his Asian neighbors achieve the same progress. It is clever propaganda because it feeds on the aftermath of the past and the mass aspirations of the present. It is well received because it is addressed to peoples already committed to socialism rather than to free enterprise.

The policy of the Soviet Union also is clever because it is designed to appeal to the aspirations of different groups in the populations. The simple appeal to Asian brotherhood, the promise of help to achieve a better life free from all the alleged shackles of the past, is good enough for the masses. And it does reach the masses. The Russians realize, as Western leaders apparently do not, that the only way to make effective contact with the unlettered masses is to go to them and to talk to them. Making many speeches each day to vast

[2] *The Nation* (Rangoon), Dec. 5, 1955.

crowds, the Soviet leaders spent a fortnight in India, traveled for thousands of miles, and preached everywhere the doctrine of neighborly assistance. The West has made no such effort to make direct contact with the Indian masses. All too often, the West seems to have acted as if it believed that all Indians could read the London *Times* or the *New York Times*.

To lure the elite groups, the Russians have a different bag of tricks. Top leaders are bombarded with friendliness and flattery. They are given lavish presents, and I do not mean a Four-H Club pin. They receive promises of economic aid in those instances, as in the case of Burmese rice exports, in which they are most urgently needed.

The intellectuals are equally the objects of subtle flattery. Groups are taken to the Soviet Union and China for extensive tours where they are treated as honored guests of the state. They are invited to make speeches, they are tendered lavish banquets, and they return impressed with the recognition they have received. Lest they seem naive in their appreciation of what they saw, it must be remembered that they did not take a Western viewpoint with them when they entered the Communist paradise. Many things that would distress a Westerner would not affect an Indian scholar simply because his political and cultural heritage is so different.

Difficulties in the Western Program

Against this formidable onslaught, the program of the West is far from successful. Economic and technical assistance is important and must be continued. But it is, at best, a clumsy instrument with which to achieve political results. It assumes that improvement in material well-being will cause people to reject Communist advances. It assumes that people will be willing to adopt desired political attitudes because of gratitude for favors given. Finally, it assumes that the slow-appearing political effects of economic improvement will have plenty of time in which to grow to healthy stature.

Actually, all these assumptions are questionable. There is no historical evidence to show that peoples ever have been politically influenced by gratitude. There is no guarantee that the degree of economic improvement that can be achieved in the foreseeable future can be sufficient to frustrate the effects of Communist propaganda among the Indian masses. We must face the possibility that we could spend millions of dollars in these aid programs without the slightest political results. As I have already said that I would not stop such aid, I must hasten to add that I believe we shall find success only by coupling these programs with other types of activity designed to have more mass appeal. I shall return to this problem later.

Another Western difficulty, much exploited by Soviet propagandists, is our failure, as the Indians see it, to take a clear-cut and definite stand on matters involving moral principle. Our ambivalent stand on colonialism is frequently cited. So, too, is our failure to make a sweeping condemnation of South African racialism. It may seem odd to us that the Soviet Union, forever ready to use any and all means to accomplish a desired end, should be regarded by anyone as setting an example in matters involving moral principles. But however strange it may seem, such is the case, and the Soviet Union has exploited with great skill its international positions on matters dear to the hearts of the Asian peoples.

Although we are filled with righteous wrath over this effort to exploit our difficulties and dilemmas, we have not succeeded in bringing to the masses the effective answers that we frequently have. We point out to our own peoples, who know it already, the credit side of our ledger, but we do not reach those whom the Soviet propaganda was designed to influence.

Many people have commented in the past on the inability of the West to state its ideological case simply, understandably, appealingly, and affirmatively. Constantly placed on the defensive by Soviet attack, the West has been inarticulate in terms meaningful to the masses. We allow free enterprise to be denounced as a cloak for exploitation. Our political democracy is too far removed from the experience or the aspirations of the people. Our standards of living are admired but regarded as unattainable in such crowded lands. Freedom and dignity for the individual—these also are claimed by the Soviet system, and we have not been effective in making the Asian masses understand the difference between Soviet theory and Soviet practice in this respect.

Finally, the West is at a disadvantage in competing with the Soviet Union because of certain obstacles created by mass attitudes at home. Let us assume for the sake of illustration the hypothesis that the present administration in Washington had reached the decision that it would be desirable, as a means of influencing Asian opinion, to support the admission of Red China to the United Nations. Such a decision could not be carried out without a political explosion of thermonuclear proportions. In a similar situation, the Soviet Government could use its control over all media of communication, blame the earlier position on Beria, and calmly announce the new policy. As an actual illustration, consider our long delay and the wrangling in Congress over the Indian request for wheat to combat the starvation caused by the Bengal famine. By contrast, when the Indian Government made a similar appeal to the Soviet Union, the affirmative response was almost instantaneous. The Soviet Union could reverse its position and make a deal in 1939 with Hitler. When Sir Samuel Hoare ran counter to British public opinion by his agreement with Monsieur Laval over Ethiopia, he failed to weather the storm and had to resign.

This, to be sure, is merely one of the inescapable consequences of political democracy and a free press. Although we would not have it otherwise, we should be less than frank if we did not admit that it is occasionally a handicap

when we are contending with a government that is not re-
sponsive to such mass pressures from its own citizens. But
we do have a right to demand of our own officials that they
refuse to sacrifice obvious and long-range national interests
merely because they find it easier to give in to a vociferous
minority or because they expect to derive partisan popularity
from the decision.

Asian Neutralism

It should be clear from these comments that I have no
great feeling of satisfaction or optimism over our efforts
to date to check the infiltration of Soviet influence into Southern Asia. Present leadership in this region is able, devoted
to public welfare, and determined to bring progress without
Communism. But I am alarmed, as I look ahead, to see how
little we have done, by comparison with our opponents, to
place ourselves *en rapport* either with the leaders or the
masses.

The Soviet approach, on the other hand, is to assure the
Asian leaders that they can count on Soviet sympathy and assistance in their great struggle toward national improvement.
Meanwhile, the masses are being cultivated with great care.
To the degree that the leaders establish close *rapport* with
the Russians, they lose their ability to take strong measures
to restrict and combat the activities of local Communist
parties. If, for example, the Indian-Soviet *rapprochement* becomes closer, how can Congress Party candidates say to the
voters: "Vote for me and not for my opponent because he
is a Communist"? To the degree that the masses identify
their aspirations with close Indo-Soviet ties, the way is being
prepared for the election of future leaders who may be less
wary of enticements of the Soviet Union than the present
generation. Obviously, the Russians do not believe that a
Nehru or an U Nu will become Communist or that they
will be unseated, either through ballots or bullets, by Com-

munists. But the Soviet tactics look ahead to a time when other, and perhaps more tractable, men will be at the helm. It is for this reason that the Russians have been most careful to avoid any criticisms of Asian neutralism.

Our own policies have been guided with less foresight. We have been bitterly critical of Asian neutralism, and our general attitude has been that other states are either with us or against us. The Indian rejoinder is simple and unequivocal. They say: "We will not accept your thesis that if we are to be your friends, we must regard as our enemies those whom you regard as your enemies. We wish to be friendly with all nations, including our Asian neighbors, as well as the Western powers."

Our opposition to neutralism overlooks the fact that even if the Asian leaders had wished to do so, they would have had enormous difficulty in persuading their peoples to accept any alignment with the West. This would not have been because the alignment was anti-Communist but because it was pro-Western. Coming so soon after emancipation from Western domination, such an alignment would have been interpreted as a submission to a new form of Western influence. There has been much resentment in India over our failure to grasp this point.

Our opposition to neutralism also overlooks the Indian determination to bend all efforts toward national development. Leaders believe that any participation in what they call "power blocs" would divert national energies away from the immediate and primary tasks of social and economic improvement. They are quick to point out that in this respect they are following the example set by the United States for many decades after it became independent.

If I have dwelt unduly long on some of the current problems in Indian relations with the East and the West, it is because they offer such a pertinent case study of present-day influences of mass attitudes and aspirations on international relations. They illustrate the folly of attempting to develop foreign policies that do not take these newly important forces into account. They indicate, at least to me, the dismal conclusion that our democracies of the West have been less skillful in this respect than our ruthless and totalitarian opponents. We shall wear badly the mantle of Western leadership if we cling to a false sense of security, adopt slogans rather than policies, and persist in the notion that all other peoples must look on us as we look on ourselves. Above all, we shall fail if we continue to assume that we can either patronize the East or deal with it just as we deal with other states of the West. In a world in which all these new forces so greatly affect relations among states, what are the prospects for world order? Such a question can be approached only by attempting to point out some of the problems that must find at least partial solution before we can begin to think or talk intelligently about any kind of a world order.

Problems of World Order

Let me say at the outset that I am not greatly interested in the mechanics of a world order. Schemes for international federation will continue to be hatched so long as there are men whose idealism is untarnished by familiarity with the lessons of history. Such schemes provide interesting intellectual exercise and a modern outlet for missionary zeal, but that is all. At our stage in the history of the state system, confronted by these great changes in international affairs, changes brought on by the effects of the new technology, the new clash of warring ideologies, and the new level of mass aspirations, the only proper concern of sensible men is with the study of conditions that must be precedent to an improvement in international relations. We ought to be concerned, not with the requirements of a world order, but with the circumstances that will bring a *détente,* a relaxation of tension, a lessening of fear. No world order can grow in our present climate. If we have a more favorable climate, the problem of a world order will take care of itself.

Obviously, the first, and an ideal, requirement would be that all peoples live under governments that are freely of their own choosing, and that all governments refrain from ideological crusades or from the use of ideologies as a means of imperialist expansion. To say this is about as revealing as to hear a candidate for political office say that he stands on a platform of honesty and prosperity.

Ultimately, however, there must be some kind of mutual understanding among the nations on the terms of coexistence. It may be implicit and unrecognized in any document that can be filed in the archives, but the sense of it must be mutually understood. Undoubtedly, it will not be wholly to our liking because our first preference would be for the disappearance of communism, and our second preference would be for a Soviet Union restricted to its prewar frontiers. Undoubtedly, it will not be to the full liking of the Soviet leaders because their ideological creed is based on the world-wide triumph of communism. But we must assume that both sides will shrink from a gigantic test of strength in order to make their most cherished aims prevail. Therefore, unless they drift into such a major conflict as a result of Soviet probing techniques in uncommitted countries, there must gradually develop some kind of mutual understanding between the Eastern and the Western worlds.

Any such trend has been greatly impeded by the legacies of the last war, notably the division of Germany, the dangerous tension in the Middle East, and the Southern Asian ferment among the masses, which could not fail to invite Soviet attention. Progress toward such an understanding has been aided by the stabilization of Western Europe, the continued prosperity of the United States, and a developing military situation that has reduced the likelihood of direct conflict.

On balance, therefore, there seems little prospect of much mutual understanding between the two great clusters of opponents in the near future. Indeed, it will never come so long as the social and political instability in Asia and Africa remain such a lodestone for Soviet imperialism. But until it does come, it is futile to talk of world order.

The second requisite is better mutual understanding between the West and the non-Western peoples outside the Iron Curtain. We must learn to understand and accept the principle of Asian neutralism and, instead of trying to coerce or persuade these peoples into close association with us, we must do what we can to strengthen them in their chosen position so that they will not be drawn gradually into the Soviet orbit.

We shall succeed in accomplishing this objective only if we can build a more satisfactory cultural relationship with the peoples concerned. We must come to understand that there is no room in the modern world for Western feelings of superiority over the East or for Eastern superiority over the West. We must come to have a man-to-man and a nation-to-nation relationship as equals, laboring together in the endless task of enabling all men to gain for themselves the best life that human society is capable of providing. Brought up as we are in the traditions of education oriented toward Western Europe and our cultural heritage from Europe, we must now learn more of the East and its ancient culture. We know so little of these lands where men lived and wrote and built temples and speculated about the universe at a time when our lands were still savage and primitive.

It is my own feeling that we can do more to stem the Soviet advance in Asia through cultural collaboration and the fostering of mutual understanding than through economic and technical assistance. The one can be reciprocal and it builds a sense of mutuality and obligation. The other becomes too easily a donor-recipient relationship.

This is another way of saying that the foundations of any future world order are to be found in the minds of men, not merely the minds of their leaders but of the masses as well. These foundations will not be laid down by force because today the weaker nations are in some ways stronger than their strong neighbors. They can be courted by both antagonists, and their charms do not diminish with the passage of time. The foundations will not be laid down by money except in so far as its intelligent use will cause men to be more rational and less desperate in their choices. The foundations will begin to appear when, and only when, the men of different nations learn what the men of great democratic societies have already learned about each other, which is that their differences must be made less meaningful than their similarities, and that none can be safe or prosper except as all are safe and prosperous. This is the lesson of the shrunken globe. It is the lesson of the Sermon on the Mount. It is not a pious exhortation but a categorical imperative. It is the price not of contentment but of survival.

2

Science, Technology and International Relations

HARRISON S. BROWN[1]

For the greater part of man's history and his prehistory, human society has been essentially static. Seldom during the million or so years of human existence has the rate of modification of man's pattern of life been so rapid that individuals have been aware of a change. In the main, persons have lived and died much as their fathers and grandfathers lived and died before them. And their children and grandchildren in turn have been destined to follow very much the same pattern of existence.

At extremely rare intervals, new discoveries or changed physical and biological environments have brought about major changes in ways of life. The controlled use of fire and the use of stone tools, for example, changed men's lives by extending the range of habitable climate, by extending the range of things that could be eaten, and by increasing the probability of recovery following a catastrophe. At a considerably later date the inventions of agriculture and of animal domestication profoundly affected men's lives by making it possible for as many as three thousand persons to be supported on land that previously had supported only one person.

Although these developments had an enormous effect upon society, it seems unlikely that much change was noticeable from one generation to the next, even during the period of most rapid spread of the use of fire, or in the period of most rapid spread of the techniques of agriculture.

[1] Professor of Geochemistry, California Institute of Technology.

Habit, [said William James] is the enormous flywheel of society . . . it alone prevents the hardest and most repulsive walks of life from being deserted by those brought up to tread therein. It keeps the fisherman and the deckhand at sea throughout the winter; it holds the miner in his darkness, and nails the countryman to his log cabin and his lonely farm throughout the months of snow. It dooms us all to fight out the battle of life on the lines of our nurture or our early choice, and to make the best of a pursuit that disagrees because there is no other for which we are fitted and it is too late to begin again.[2]

It seems clear that largely as a result of the force of habit, the time scale for major changes in ways of life in our society must usually be measured by the number of years that separate one generation from the next, rather than in shorter intervals of one, two or three years—or even a decade. In addition, we must remember that a person's opinions concerning a variety of important matters are usually formulated during the earlier years of life, while in most societies positions of influence and power are usually not attained until later years. This has had a stabilizing influence that has tended to maintain the *status quo,* with the result that the rate of social change must often be measured on a time scale far longer than the interval that separates the birth of one generation from that of the next. Thus had it not been for the historian or for the stories told in songs and legend that were passed from one generation to the next, most men throughout human history would have been unaware that their ways of life were appreciably different from those of their remote ancestors.

I have prefaced my discussion with these brief statements concerning time scale, for the reason that its importance in the web of events that is determining the future of our nation—and for that matter, the future of the human species—is all too little appreciated, often with unfortunate consequences.

[2] William James, *The Principles of Psychology* (1905), Vol. 1, p. 121.

The Scientific Revolution

During the last 300 years, man's way of life has changed at a rate that is probably unprecedented in the million or so years of his existence. In this interval of time, which has been well termed the "Scientific Revolution," man has attained a remarkable degree of control over his environment. Through the achievement of a partial understanding of how nature operates, he has learned how to grow more crops on a given piece of land; he has learned a great deal about disease and how to control it; he has learned how to harness the energy of fossil fuels; he has learned how to transport his ideas, himself, and his goods rapidly over long distances.

One result of these innovations has been to accelerate the spread of agriculture over the world. A second result has been to shift man in many parts of the world from a predominantly rural existence within the framework of an agricultural economy to a predominantly urban existence within the framework of an industrial economy. A third result has been to stimulate increasing individual demands for material possessions. A fourth result has been to stimulate an unprecedented rate of increase of human population.

In the first 5,000 to 10,000 years of the agricultural revolution, the population of the world increased perhaps thirty to forty fold. In the first 300 years of the scientific revolution, the population has already increased about five-fold and thus far there is not the slightest evidence of a slackening. Indeed, not only has the population been increasing rapidly since the middle of the seventeenth century, but the annual rate of increase has been growing rapidly as well.

Thus far the United States has gone farther along the path of applying science and technology to the task of increasing productivity than has any other nation. During the past hundred years our per-capita flow of goods and associated with it our per-capita consumption of energy and other raw materials have increased steadily. We have now reached the point where in order to maintain our present productivity we have well over eight tons of steel in use for every person in our country—steel in the form of machines, automobiles, ships, nails, and a variety of other tools and products such as are needed in a highly industrialized society.

In order to keep our society and with it our eight tons of steel per person operating, we consume energy at a rate equivalent to burning about eight tons of coal per person per year. In general it appears that the energy contained in a ton of coal is required each year in order to keep a ton of steel functioning in a modern industrial society.

We use large quantities of metals in addition to steel, among them copper, aluminum, manganese, chromium, tin, and lead. We must mine each year vast tonnages of ores for the purpose of creating new metal capital and of replacing metals that have been lost. We require each year vast quantities of nonmetals, such as stone and gravel for building and roads, sulfur for sulfuric acid and phosphate rock for fertilizers. In order to support a single person in our country, over twenty tons of raw materials must be mined, quarried, processed and transported each year.

Today we are confronted by diminishing grades of raw materials in many areas of industrial activity. For example, only a few decades ago we were mining copper ore that contained 5 per cent copper. Today our average copper ore contains only 0.6 per cent of the metal. Undoubtedly in the years ahead we shall be mining ores that contain even smaller concentrations of the element. From the point of view of technology, this is something well within the realm of feasibility—but at a price. In order to extract copper from ores of still lower grade, we must pour more technology into the system; we must move and process larger quantities of ore per unit of production; we must use more machinery and consume more energy. In short, extraction of copper from lower grades of ore requires using increased amounts of steel and other metals and, associated with its use, increased energy consumption.

No matter where we turn in our considerations of critical metals, we encounter similar situations. Where once we processed only high grade iron ores, we now find ourselves processing lower grade taconites. Where once we processed only high grade domestic bauxite for aluminum, we now find ourselves starting to process the more difficult-to-handle aluminum-bearing clays. We find ourselves drilling ever deeper for oil, mining at lower and lower depths, and transporting water over greater and greater distances. All of this means ever-larger quantities of steel and other metals in use —and as a corollary, ever-greater energy consumption per unit of industrial output.

We can of course import raw materials instead of, or in addition to, processing lower grade domestic ores. And indeed we now find ourselves investing in projects for obtaining iron ore from Labrador, Liberia, and Venezuela. Our imports of petroleum from the Middle East and from South America are steadily increasing. We import manganese from India, copper from Peru, and bauxite from Jamaica. But we must remember that in order to import these materials, we must expend large quantities of materials and energy for the construction and the operation of the necessary transportation facilities. In many cases the additional consumption of materials and energy that would be involved in importing the raw material approaches the additional consumption required to obtain the material from lower grade domestic ore.

No matter how we look at the situation, we must conclude that our consumption of energy and other raw materials per unit of output must continue to increase with time. When we couple this with the fact that per-capita demands for goods are still increasing, and with the even more important fact that our population is increasing more rapidly than that of most nations, it seems likely that our demands for raw materials in the years ahead will pale those of today into insignificance.

At the present time, for example, the per-capita amount of steel in use in the United States is increasing at the rate of about 0.3 tons per year. By 1975 there may well be nearly fifteen tons of steel in use per person. When we consider the likelihood that by 1975 our population may be 225 millions, the total amount of steel in use may then have reached 3.4 billion tons. Demands for other metals and for energy will be correspondingly much higher than they are today. And those demands must be filled in a world where grades of ore are becoming progressively poorer and where competition for raw materials is becoming progressively more keen.

Spread of Industrialization

During the last three centuries, we have seen the emergence of industrialization in England, and we have seen it spread throughout Western Europe. In the last 150 years, we have seen industrialization cross the Atlantic and spread over North America. In the last sixty years, we have seen industrialization cross the Pacific to Japan. In the last thirty-five years, we have seen it spread to the Soviet Union. Today, we can observe it spreading to Australia and to parts of Africa. We can also hear rumblings of impending industrialization in India, in China, in other regions of southeast Asia, and in regions of South America.

It seems to me that in the absence of a world catastrophe this spread of industrialization to the rest of the world is inevitable, in the same sense that the spread of agriculture throughout the world was inevitable, once agriculture was invented. It seems unlikely that industrialized and unindustrialized nations can coexist indefinitely any more than the agricultural and food-gathering cultures of the past were able to coexist indefinitely once agriculture started its inexorable spread.

In addition, it seems clear that the further spread of industrialization necessarily must take place within a framework that differs considerably from the framework within which industrialization has thus far spread throughout the western world. One of the primary reasons for this is that the ratios of people to available land, and of people to readily accessible resources, are much larger now than they were then.

To what levels can we expect the large and crowded areas of Asia eventually to industrialize? I believe that in the absence of a world catastrophe the process of industrialization will continue until per-capita consumption of metals and energy reaches levels that are at least as high as the per-capita levels that prevail in the West today. I say this in spite of the fact that many of my Asian friends maintain that only a small fraction of Western productivity will suffice for India and China.

Last year I had the opportunity of spending several months in India, and while I was there, I was told repeatedly that although India had embarked on an industrialization program, there was no intention of attempting to achieve Western levels of productivity. When I asked about their aims, I was told that they were attempting only to reach a level of productivity at which the average Indian could live out his natural life span, at which he could have enough to eat, a roof over his head, some clothing, and the opportunity of raising his children in a decent environment. It was invariably stressed that they had no desire for our Western luxuries. It was quite clear that they believed that most Western productivity was aimed at the production of nonessential goods.

I attempted to stress that when one spoke in terms of making it possible for the average person to live out the normal life span with which he was endowed, one necessarily had to speak in terms of per-capita levels of productivity approaching those that exist in the West. In order to lessen mortality, it is first necessary to produce more food. India has reached the point at which food production can be increased appreciably only by extensive application of the results of modern science and technology. It must resort to the wide-spread use of fertilizers and other agricultural chemicals. In order to produce the necessary fertilizers and chemicals, India needs elaborate plants, which in turn require substantial quantities of steel and other metals for their construction. It needs more roads, railroad lines, trucks, and trains in order to transport raw materials, fertilizers, and food.

On the public health side, a substantial decrease in mortality would require vast numbers of hospitals and plants for the production of antibiotics and other pharmaceuticals. It would require more education, which would in turn necessitate more schools, more books, more equipment. In short, we find that with the single goal of reducing mortality to something approaching Western levels, something approaching Western levels of industrialization would be required. Although it would not be necessary to have eight tons of steel in use per person, it would be difficult to get by with much less than one or two tons.

We may now ask: How rapidly can we expect industrialization to spread to the rest of the world? Here we can obtain some idea from the experience already achieved by industrialized countries. The United States, for example, has been able to double its pig iron production every ten years or so for very long periods of time. For many years Japan succeeded in doubling pig iron production every five years. The Soviet Union maintained a doubling time of about five years until the outbreak of the Second World War.

India is today one of the major steel producers of Asia, but its production has thus far increased at a very slow rate.

It required twenty-six years for India to double its pig iron production after 1924. Nevertheless, when we look at the picture of India's resources and at its industrialization program, it seems clear that India should be able to achieve a doubling time for pig iron production of about ten years and to maintain that rate of increase for a very long period of time. India has magnificent reserves of high-grade iron-ore—perhaps the finest in the world—and although it is short of coal of metallurgical grade, there are technological tricks for circumventing this difficulty. And although India's per-capita coal reserves are far smaller than those that are characteristic of the major industrial powers of the West, it has sufficient coal to permit it to double pig iron production several times before it is in danger of running out of fuel. By that time, we can be confident, India can be in a position to utilize nuclear energy for both pig iron and steel production.

At the present time India is producing pig iron at a rate of 1.8 million tons per year. Plans have been made to increase the capacity of the steel industry during the next few years: a new plant is being built by a West German firm and another by the Soviet Union. An American firm has contracted to increase the capacity of the largest existing installation. It seems likely that the British will construct still another plant. If all of these plans are realized, the output of finished steel may reach 4.5 million tons annually by 1960-61 and pig iron production might reach 6 million tons. The steel program necessitates a stepping up of the coal output from the present level of 37 million tons to 60 million tons.

If we can make the reasonable assumption that India is able to achieve and maintain a ten-year doubling time for at least a few decades following 1960, then pig iron production would reach about 15 million tons by 1975, and about 80 million tons by the year 2000. By that time about 2 billion tons of pig iron would have been produced, or about 5 tons per person living in India in 1955. But when we take into account the losses of iron involved in the steel cycle and the fact that the population of India is increasing rapidly, we see that only a fraction of that quantity would actually be used. We are thus forced to the conclusion that even with a doubling time of ten years, at least a half century would be required for India to achieve a level of per-capita productivity such as existed in Japan immediately prior to the Second World War. The chances are great that an even longer time will be required.

Thus we see that in the absence of a new concept—of a new working principle—the levels of living in the heavily populated areas of Asia will not be elevated rapidly—especially when we view the time scale in terms of the length of the human life. This means of course that even in the face of rapid progress such as we have here envisaged, there will be discontent and strong feelings that productivity should be increased even more rapidly.

Future Technological Changes

Associated with an increased tempo of industrialization, we can foresee a number of technological changes that will greatly affect the relationships between nations. We must ask: What are the most important of these changes likely to be?

We can look forward in the years ahead to considerable improvements in our knowledge of materials and how to process them. We shall probably develop metals that can withstand far more severe stresses and strains over greater temperature ranges than can existing alloys. We shall develop a greater variety of useful nonmetallic substances, particularly plastics. Aircraft will probably be developed that can carry heavy loads half-way around the world in a few hours. Continued development of automation and computers will make possible new processes and new products and a steadily increasing output of goods per man-hour. Transportation and communications systems will become increasingly complex. Man's ability to destroy will continue to increase. His ability to defend himself will increase, but not so rapidly as his ability to destroy.

As production increases and as population increases, our rate of consumption of raw materials will increase, and it will be necessary for us to obtain our raw materials from progressively leaner ores. In order to do this, it will be necessary to put more and more technology into the system, and in turn it will be necessary for us to bring into use increasing per-capita quantities of metals and other substances.

So long as there is an ample supply of energy, we shall be able to process extremely low grade substances in order to obtain the raw materials we need. As grades move downward, increasing emphasis will be placed upon the isolation of by-products and co-products, and eventually we may reach the time when as many as twenty to thirty products are obtained from the single operation of "mining" ordinary rock. As grade goes down, energy costs per unit of output will of course go up, but given adequate supplies of energy, it will be possible for industry to be fed for a very long time from the leanest of substances.

As man travels along the road that will lead eventually to his processing such substances as granitic rock and sea-water, he will process a sequence of substances of intermediate grade. He will isolate iron from taconites, aluminum from anorthosites and clays, produce sulfuric acid from calcium sulfate, and isolate copper, tin, lead, nickel, and germanium from a variety of very low grade deposits. But ultimately he will derive his sustenance from the leanest of materials—the ordinary rocks of the earth's crust and the waters of the sea.

The question what constitutes an available mineral resource is essentially a question of energy. As time goes on energy consumption per unit of industrial consumption must necessarily increase. As per-capita consumption, population, and the extent of industrialized areas increase, total energy consumption must increase even more sharply. Are there adequate sources of energy available to us that can be tapped?

Fortunately nature has placed at our disposal huge reservoirs of energy. We know that if necessary, the sun's rays can be harnessed directly to produce mechanical power. We know that useful power can be produced from uranium and thorium, and we know that sufficient quantities of these substances are available in the earth's minerals and rocks to keep a world civilization operating at a high level of productivity for many millenia. We know that in some regions of the world there are large quantities of coal and petroleum that have not yet been tapped. It seems clear that given the trained man power, the imagination, and the research, man has at his disposal ample supplies of energy.

Nevertheless, it seems equally clear that there will be considerable dislocation as various parts of the world shift from one energy source to another. We shall notice this particularly during the next few decades when tremendous changes will take place in the petroleum picture. It now seems quite plausible, for example, that the United States will pass through its peak of petroleum production within a few years of 1965. The peak of world petroleum production should be reached by the turn of the century.

As petroleum and oil shales dwindle, liquid fuels will be produced by coal hydrogenation. As coal in turn dwindles, its use will be confined to premium functions, and the use of atomic energy will increase rapidly. Indeed, it now seems likely that atomic energy will come into use in the very near future in several regions of the world that today are short of conventional energy sources.

The world food picture is far less bright than the energy picture. In principle the world can produce considerably more food than it is producing at the present time. But major increases will require the application of an enormous amount of technology, a great deal of capital investment, and the dissemination of modern agricultural knowledge throughout the world. Fertilizer production must be greatly increased; vast irrigation systems must be constructed; a variety of agricultural chemicals must be produced; people must be taught modern agricultural techniques. All of this, of course, is possible. But it is difficult to envisage its being done quickly.

Impact on International Relations

Let us now apply the conclusions we have reached thus far to an attempt to forecast the broad future pattern of developments involving science, technology, and the relationships between nations. Please note that I have used the word *forecast* rather than prophesy. For one thing, I realize that prophets are traditionally stoned. But the main reason involves the fact that there are many possible patterns of future development. All we can do is look at the world about us to the best of our ability and choose the most likely of those patterns, much as the weatherman looks at the data available to him and then chooses the most likely of the possible weather patterns. Needless to say, and perhaps fortunately, our chances of being wrong concerning these matters are even greater than the chances of our finding that the weatherman has erred in a forecast.

As we have seen, we are living in a world characterized by the rapid spread of industrialization, by increasing per-capita demands for raw materials, by increasing population, and by decreasing availability of high grade raw materials. Clearly, as time goes by, either it will be necessary for each industrial country to expend a great deal of technology in order to extract its raw materials from relatively low grade ores, or it will be necessary for it to import these materials.

We can expect that competition between nations for the earth's resources will become increasingly keen. But resource depletion will eventually become the great leveler of nations, and most of the major industrial areas of the world will eventually find it easier to gain their sustenance by applying science and technology to the task of processing domestic, low grade substances than to look abroad.

The depletion of resources will make it more and more difficult for the less-developed areas of the world to obtain the materials they need for their own industrialization. Increasing difficulty of importation will necessitate the application of an ever greater amount of technology to their own industrialization problems. Indeed, it seems likely that we are approaching the interesting situation in which the less developed and more impoverished an area is, the higher is the level of technology required to achieve and maintain an adequate standard of living. For these reasons, the industrialization of the unindustrialized parts of the world will become more difficult with each passing year.

Standards of living will probably not improve as rapidly as industrialization spreads for the reason that although human beings are relatively slow breeders, when compared with other members of the animal kingdom, they are nevertheless amazingly persistent in their breeding habits. Techniques for death control are usually adopted fairly quickly in practically all societies, but there appears to be little inclination to regulate the number of human beings.

Man's lack of inclination to regulate his numbers is frequently blamed on the fact that he has no magic method for doing this. We often hear that if only we had a little pill that would produce temporary sterility, the problem would be solved. Although I personally believe that it is important that such a pill be developed, I doubt that its use would spread on a time scale much shorter than a generation or two. In any event, I sadly doubt that it would have much effect in decreasing the enormous rate of population increase that is generally associated with the initial stages of industrialization.

Thus it seems likely that in the absence of our bringing something new into the picture, the process of industrialization in the underdeveloped areas of the world will be characterized more by increasing numbers of people than by a rapid improvement in the standards of living.

Two factors will make it increasingly difficult for underdeveloped areas to industrialize within the framework of democratic institutions. We have already noted that the slowness of the industrialization process together with rapidly increasing numbers of people pressing heavily on available food is likely to breed misery, impatience, and discontent. The surplus people will flock to the mushrooming cities, and it is in the cities that the misery and the discontent are likely to breed uprisings and violence. It is in this kind of atmosphere that totalitarianism can spread over the greater part of the earth.

In the years ahead the industrialized areas themselves will be subjected to continuously increasing pressures that can lead to the progressive deterioration and destruction of democratic institutions. As populations become larger, as it becomes increasingly difficult to extract our sustenance from the earth, as there emerges a growing awareness concerning the vulnerability of industrial society to disruption, there will emerge greater and greater pressures for increased efficiency, for more elaborate organization and for regimentation in practically all levels of our culture. Indeed, we can see this process taking place today, at various rates, in most Western nations—including the United States.

And in this connection we must remember that our science and our technology have converted the road that leads to totalitarianism into a one-way street. Today the rulers of totalitarian states have available tools of both coercion and persuasion of unprecedented power—tools undreamed of by our ancestors. No longer is it possible for people to revolt against their oppressors using simple weapons such as stones, sticks and muskets. Once totalitarian power is achieved, it cannot be overthrown in the absence of outside forces—the tools for its perpetuation are too powerful.

The free world will be affected by further aspects of the movement toward world-wide industrialization. We have already seen that there will be increasing competition for raw materials. Further, as nations that are at present unindustrialized become industrialized, they will acquire for themselves the power to manufacture the instruments of war. We saw what happened in 1941 when a recently industrialized Japan acquired that power. We also see what is happening today now that a recently industrialized Soviet Union has acquired an even greater power. And in the absence of a sound policy, we can guess what might happen when China acquires the power of producing its own instruments of war and ceases to be dependent on Soviet sources of supply.

Atomic energy is bound to play an extremely important role in all of the considerations I have thus far mentioned. At least three nations now have it within their power to manufacture atomic bombs. Two nations have produced thermonuclear explosions, and a third will have H-bombs in a few months.

Hand in hand with the spread of atomic power, there will emerge the ability to manufacture ingredients for atomic bombs and, eventually, H-bombs. Today there are government-sponsored groups working on atomic energy in many of the nations of the world, ranging from the nations of Western Europe to many of the nations of Asia, including India, Pakistan, the Philippines, and Japan. Soon we shall observe the production of electricity from atomic energy in many of these areas, and not long after that time, we may well observe the production of stockpiles of atomic weapons. The effects of these developments on the relations between nations will certainly be of enormous scope. And much to my own personal dismay, all of these developments are taking place in the presence of international chaos and in the absence of anything approaching international control over the means for producing atomic death and destruction.

This brings up the question: How vulnerable are industrialized nations to atomic attack? As I look over the United States with its complex network of mines, industrial plants and transportation—and as I come more and more to appreciate the extent to which our survival depends on the smooth functioning of that network—I realize that we are probably much more vulnerable to atomic attack than we think. I do not believe that many hydrogen bombs would be required so to disrupt our industrial network that it would stop functioning. Indeed, I seriously doubt that modern industrial society could recover from the effects of an "all-out" war in which our modern methods of mass destruction are widely used.

Clearly, in the years ahead there will be steady, and relatively speaking rapid, change in the international environment—a change being brought about by science and technology. Nations that are now the most powerful will no longer be so powerful. Nations that have been unable, independently, to threaten war will be able to wage it. Nations that have been poor will become, relatively speaking, well off. Some nations that have been rich will become, relatively speaking, less well off.

This rapidly changing scene will present enormous problems to the United States. How can we preserve in the years ahead our standard of living and our democratic way of life in the face of the tremendous forces that are working in the direction of destroying them?

I doubt that anyone of us knows the answers—certainly I do not know. Yet, I believe that it is possible for us to solve these problems. But solution is possible only if we are willing to look into the future and to take the long view rather than just the day-to-day short one. If we are willing to do this—to face the future squarely and to apply our imagination and our genius to these problems—then I believe that there is a finite chance that we shall leave our children a world that is at least as habitable as that which we inherited from our parents. But if we refuse to look squarely at the future and to recognize these problems, I fear that our civilization will perish, and we may descend into another, and perhaps permanent, Age of Darkness.

3

Conflicts Arising Out of Differing Governmental and Political Institutions

DENIS W. BROGAN[1]

AFTER the First World War, Marshal Foch confessed that he no longer admired Napoleon as much as he once had. The Emperor had been the God of his idolatry, but was at last seen as not quite so divine. Why? Not simply because Foch had himself been a victorious commander and put himself on an equal with his teacher, but because Foch had commanded an allied coalition and had learned, the hard way, how difficult it was to keep allied armies together; and thus how comparatively easy was the task of the commander of unified political forces, like Napoleon and, one may say, of the recently undeified Stalin.

I have recalled this anecdote of Foch because it illustrates the difficulty that I shall deal with in this lecture. That difficulty arises essentially out of the task of keeping together any political alliance of free peoples, which necessarily means an alliance of free voters, products of political systems differing in origin, in mechanical organization, in age, in national priorities and, the further to confuse, too often agreeing only verbally.

Major Difficulties in Collaboration

There is nothing odd or diabolical or the product of conspiracy in recurring friction between bodies politic that are agreed on one great fundamental. Perhaps that unity on one

[1] Professor of Political Science, Cambridge University, and Fellow of Peterhouse.

37

fundamental should dominate everything else, like love in the first fine careless rapture of the beginning of the affair. What we have to deal with in our time, however, is neither the beginning nor the end of the affair, but the middle term of satisfactory, loyal, permanent matrimony—and that such an honorable estate automatically provides harmony and constant agreement is a dream of felicity believed in only by romantic novelists of the old school and by June brides in the advertising sections of the shiny magazines.

We can take it for granted then, that all alliances, coalitions, or associations of powers or peoples involve friction over means, and even over all ends, but the one unifying aim that brought about and kept the alliance in existence. That aim, in so far as it effects the Western alliance, we can, I suppose, identify as "freedom"; and the very ambiguity of the term, which I shall have to refer to more than once, suggests some of the difficulties confronting any free coalition.

As a preliminary, we must take account of two illusions that make political collaboration difficult between closely linked political societies. The first is the optimistic belief that the equivalent of a world public opinion already exists, that the verbal ways of appeal that are assumed to be effective inside a defined national community are equally or nearly equally effective in appealing to another nation or another group of nations. It is not necessarily foolish to believe this in some situations. There may be in certain areas of political conduct that common public to which appeals can be made, as they can be made inside unified national societies. Thus one society, the American, and another, the British, have certain traditions in common, certain habits of political argument in common that it would be time wasting to ignore. At times, societies that have no such common traditions may be thrown together by a common interest, usually a common danger, and for that time political collaboration may be, or as is more often the case may seem to be, easy.

But these common ways of political discourse, these occasions of spontaneous collaboration are rare, and it is the part of political prudence to assume that they can normally be disregarded and that each sovereign state is cut off from its neighbors more than it is united to them; and that collaboration is going to be difficult. It will be difficult not only in ways that make collaboration difficult inside nations but also in ways that arise from the fact that the nation state, for all its imperfections and dangers, does create the habits of cooperation that so far exist only in embryo among the peoples of different nation states.

The second illusion is that there exists among nations a common national memory such as serves as a cement inside a national society. Quarrels inside a nation may be bitter family quarrels, and they may breed internal discord, but there is, even in a divided nation, an understanding of the dividing passions that can seldom be found among nations, even between friendly nations. Thus political methods that work successfully, or at any rate do not fail completely, inside a national society may be quite irrelevant among nations and sometimes may be highly dangerous.

These two illusions must be continuously borne in mind while our attention is directed to the special difficulties caused by the differences bred by various political structures and methods. Indeed, often the difficulties that at first sight seem to be caused by different political institutions or habits turn out, on examination, to be merely special cases of the two illusions. Thus the adoption by one country of the political structure of another or the creation of world organization may disappoint hopes simply because the basic difficulties are unaffected. There is no common body politic, only common devices; there is no common memory, only a common set of problems and inherited difficulties. Even an agreement on common remedies may not breed really easy and confident co-operation because there is a different order of national priorities. Every nation may agree in its total list of aims, even agree on the methods of solution, yet co-operation may be difficult simply because the order of national priorities is different. And as all things cannot be done at the same time, the effort of one nation to choose to do one thing first and another to do something else first may produce as much confusion as differences in ends or means. No doubt they will be more manageable differences, but they may be very serious all the same.

Institutional Differences

To turn now to the specifically institutional differences. We can, I think, take it for granted that a nation will think there is one good way of doing something, which will be preferred to any other. Normally, but not uniformly, that way will be the traditional way of doing things in the country concerned; there will be a right or a wrong way or, as we say in the country where I live, an English and an un-English way of doing things.

Normally, but not always, for in a country with some good or bad reason for doubting the efficacy of its institutional equipment, there may be a naive admiration for the methods of another country, flattering but misleading. Thus a great many people in France think the solution for the political problems of the French Republic lies in an imitation of English methods, e.g. in the resort to the right of dissolution of parliament. A smaller group thinks that the remedy is the importation of the American independent presidential executive. In the United States, there are many, mainly among political scientists, who think that some adaptation of the British cabinet system or of the system of recruitment of the higher civil service, would serve to diminish certain evils in the American political system.

There may be equivalents of these critics of the domestic admirers of the imported political article in England. But, although I get around a lot, I do not seem to meet them, for as I have hinted, the deliberate importation of foreign institutions falls under the ban of being un-English, a condemnation all the more complete for being unconsciously arrogant. "Storm in Channel: Continent isolated," is not thought by most English people to be funny but merely the statement of a unfortunate state of affairs from which the Continent will suffer, and which is probably a sign of divine wrath. Applied to anything serious, "they order these matters better in France" is a deeply un-English statement. The English will, and do, frequently exemplify many of the difficulties to international co-operation provided by institutional differences and biases. But few examples will arise from the belief that the English have much to learn from others, many from two related beliefs, that foreigners have a great deal to learn but are practically incapable of learning. And if this attitude is irritating or even dangerous, at any rate it saves the English from much disappointment. They do not ask: "Why can't Johnny (or Sammy) read." They note, sadly and stiffly, that he cannot and that the reading will have to be done for him.

Perhaps the English attitude in all its purity is not quite so much an unconditioned reflex as it was. It is still a deep attitude, however, and it is the attitude of the man in the street in nearly all countries. He may not think much of the way his affairs are run by home methods, but he does not believe in any others, or in any league, coalition, or alliance using any other methods. The members of his own national society who tolerate such deviations from the normal are fools or knaves or both. The English may believe more in fools, the Americans more in knaves (I make no judgment on the relative wisdom of these attitudes); but the result is much the same. What is not done in the traditional, national way is under suspicion. Home cooking is preferred; the result may be indigestible, but it is familiar.

It would be misleading to suggest that even in the confident, united, expanding Atlantic society of a century ago, there were not serious conflicts arising from institutional differences. I shall have to return to this point later, but it is worth noting that in the early nineteenth century, the British Foreign Office did not, if one may judge by the text of treaties, fully appreciate until the eve of the Civil War the importance of the very different American method of ratifying treaties. It may be doubted, despite some educational experiences like those provided by the long history of the Isthmian Canal controversy, whether these differences were fully appreciated until the debacle of the Treaty of Versailles.

There are other difficulties. The United States was, for long, the only important republic in the world, the "last, best hope of earth" for many millions of non-Americans and the verbal patron of nations "rightly struggling to be free." This created some difficulties and would have created more if the United States had moved on from verbal to active policies, throwing it athwart Russia or Germany or Britain. The free and easy manners of parliamentary government bred, in Palmerston, habits much disliked (not always unreasonably) by powers like Austria. French foreign policy was much more bedevilled by internal politics than it is customary to recognize. More or less free governments found it difficult to get on with despotisms or even with the courtier ministers of the family alliances that still played an important role. But comparing the troubles of 1856 with those of 1956, we are inclined to say to our ancestors: "You didn't know how lucky you were. We have never had it so good."

We know this, we feel this, and we resent this. What form does this knowledge and resentment take? It takes, particularly in America, the form of a simplifying of the situation. There is in existence an alliance of free peoples, which all really free peoples—if they had any sense, gratitude, or guts—would join. That alliance of free nations has all moral and most material assets on its side. It can only be beaten if it is betrayed by inconstant allies or frightened or conniving neutrals. Let the free men, or the would-be free men, stand up and be counted—or else.

This is a simplified but not, I think, an unjust picture of a common American attitude. And behind that attitude lies a combination of the two illusions with whose nefarious effects I began my lecture. There is the assumption that there exists a unified world opinion, speaking a common moral language, and that there is a common historical world picture that will provide the necessary images, rhetoric, and channels of communication of a common purpose. This may not be true, and over a great part of the world it is certainly not true.

It was a rash assumption a hundred years ago that such a world existed or was being brought into existence by "progress" and by force. It is an absurd assumption now. It was a dangerous illusion that such a world could be given a common historical background, that Shakespeare and Magna Carta could replace the Hindu epics and the Indian social structure. It still is. For it is a truth, if a sad truth, that such unity is yet to be created and in that simple form is never likely to be created. We are still divided and in many ways it may be fortunate that we are, "lest one good custom should corrupt the world." But we are certainly divided.

Sources of Difficulties in Western Alliance

Let us look, first of all, at the Western alliance. How far are its difficulties created by institutional differences? How far are they created by verbal obstacles? It is simplest to take the second class of differences first, as many of the difficulties that arise from true institutional differences are multiplied by verbal disagreements.

Take two formal differences between Britain and the United States. Britain has a monarchial form of government and was, or possibly still is, the center of an "empire." The United States is a republic and holds imperialism in horror, except in advertising; but the popularity of terms like "empire state" and "king size" does not invalidate the fact that "republican government" means a lot to the American, and that he is often unable to identify a similar form of government because it does not meet the formal test of being republican. For example, many Americans until recently believed Canada was not a republic but was a part of an empire, and ergo was not "free." Millions believed that Canada paid "tribute" to Britain, a belief that must have withered at the news of the state of the Canadian dollar. But absurd as this belief was, it was not unimportant, and it possibly is not unimportant. For simply because of verbal differences, it may still be difficult to accept the fact that one country is really a body politic of the same kind.

More serious is the conviction that certain political habits and biases are essential elements of all free governments. Thus an astonishingly large number of Americans identify freedom with the most rigorous separation of church and state; societies that do not erect a wall as high as that the Supreme Court has professed to extract from history are not free. If this be so, my native country of Scotland would not be free, for it ignores that barrier in many ways. But the conclusion that Scotland is not a free political society, except in so far as it is exploited by England, is absurd. It would be possible but not very profitable to multiply instances of corresponding snap judgments on the other side. For example, there is a widespread European and British belief that the United States is to be judged solely by its success in solving its racial problems, and there is a refusal to see as complicated, a problem that can be dealt with so simply, at a distance, by a few simple formulae

These biases must again always be borne in mind when we are thinking of what political obstacles there are to close co-operation or even to tolerance, for they color our views or the view of the man in the street about the means as well as the ends of political institutions. We find ourselves less willing to make allowances for the differences in institutions because we are already intolerant of the ends those institutions serve, or that we innocently, and often arrogantly, assume that they serve.

The differences in the political and institutional set-up, however, are a sufficiently important obstacle to deserve having some time devoted to them. I shall deal mainly, although not exclusively, with Anglo-American examples of the differences, not only because they are of great importance in themselves, but also because I know more about them. But some of the things I have to say are applicable to a far wider field of international problems than that of Anglo-American relations. After all, the historic background in common, the political language in common, the consequent common universe of discourse, though in part a fiction, is in part a fact and more of a fact than that involved in any other assumed universe of discourse.

I have already spoken of the ambiguity or irrelevance of the terms "republic" and "monarchy," but far more serious is the ambiguity of the word "democracy." "Republic" and "monarchy" have special, definable, and defined meanings. They may be misleading. I have already dealt with the case of Canada, but we have the case of the Union of Soviet Socialist Republics. We may be convinced that this is simply the Tsardom writ large, that Ivan the Terrible and Stalin were not only alike as personalities but also held the same office. Whereas we have had for a long time, however, a suitable vocabulary for tyrants like Ivan the Terrible we have not got a suitable vocabulary for people like Stalin whom we tend to think of as a unique specimen. It may not be so now, but certainly the republican form of the Soviet state disarmed many critics in America and may disarm many more in the next few years. It is natural for Americans to think of the spread of republics—until today there are only a handful of monarchies and no monarchies of the old traditional absolute type at all—as automatically meaning progress. Perhaps it does, but the question is not yet settled, if by republic we mean simply the absence of a hereditary chief ruler.

"Democracy" is, however, the real stumbling block. For it is doubtful if "democracy" has ever meant in modern times merely a "government of the people, by the people," or has ever meant, as republic has often meant, just a form of governmental organization. Democracy has had all sorts of overtones and has included an attitude to human personality, to human rights, and to social conduct that not all free, politically speaking, societies have manifested. Thus when an American notes, with regret, that Britain is not a republic and thinks of the Commonwealth in terms of an outmoded empire, which he automatically assumes to have been a bad thing, he is not often saying anything relevant, although his illusion may be politically important.

But when he denies to Britain the character of a democracy, he is saying something not necessarily foolish, for he is pointing, however clumsily, to a real difference in the social and political structures of the two countries. He exaggerates the importance of the crown, of the hereditary aristocracy, of the established church, and of the class differences, which are underlined and—to some extent—caused by education. But he is talking, all the same, about something real, about a difference between what is still largely a "deferential" society (and so, in the American sense, an undemocratic society) and a society in many ways less egalitarian than English society, yet more "democratic" in the sense that it is less deferential, that the man in the street is the measure of all things or, at any rate, that a plausible pretense is made to suggest that he is.

This difference will find institutional form. On the whole, English education will profess to care more for the exceptional boy or girl than for the common boy or girl; it will be assumed that education is something given down rather than ordered by the parent or the child. Standards, which may be irrelevant or foolish, will be fairly easily maintained. In the United States, there will be an assumption that if Johnny can't read maybe reading isn't as important as all that, that if the old hierarchical culture isn't vendible any more, it had better be scrapped in favor of something that people really want.

In the same way, the claim of a group to acceptance of its views because it is better educated, knows more of the world, has sounder traditions, and has more sense of responsibility can be argued for in England with tact, no doubt, but not with a complete absence of confidence, while the same claims in America have to be concealed. The results may be the same. The claims of the English hierarchical groups may be less and less attended to, and it would be a very naive American who took seriously all these obeisances to the good head, as well as good heart, of the common man. But the difference remains and is important.

In a still deferential country like England, the unique responsibility of the government (to be answered for in due course to the electorate) is accepted, and that is taken for granted. Grumbled against, but accepted, is the view that all important discussion should take place in the House of Commons. Accepted without question is the unity of the executive, not the American unity in one person, but the unity of the cabinet system where it does not matter what the government says so long as all its spokesmen say the same thing.

In the United States, the concentration of all responsible

decisions in one person is tempered by the existence of rival institutions, in the forms of both houses of Congress. It is expected that the government of the United States will speak with several voices, that the debate inside the governing bodies will be public and continuous, and that it will be impossible to commit the people of the United States, except after a long and tumultuous controversy. The English people, used to the formally undivided voice of its government, is baffled, however, by so many rival voices, each speaking with authority, and the American, or European, observer of the English scene either takes for servility the apparent discipline of the governing party, or takes too seriously the formal opposition of the Opposition and is shocked to discover that once it is the Government, the Opposition speaks like a government and often very like the previous government.

It may be national bias, but it seems to me that the second type of behavior, the British, causes less mischief than the first. It is true that the dissents of the American system are often less serious than they can be made to appear and that the whole pressure of the modern world is in favor of the increasing power of the executive, that is, of the President. Again, however, peoples with a different tradition and a different historical memory cannot easily be expected to see this.

The weakness of the British attitude is the assumption, innocently and naturally made, that what suits Britain also suits the rest of the world. Never overwhelmingly powerful, Britain has been forced to pay attention to the public opinion of the outside world. Britain, however, has often thought of such opinion as that of obstinately backward children who really deserve the cane, but have to be reasoned with—and reasoned with in the English manner. This British attitude is not institutionalized, but the American attitude is. Partly this is due to the deeply and, I think, excessively legal character given to American politics by the role of the courts in political matters. Problems that in Britain are reduced to problems of conduct, of playing the game (which must be cricket not baseball, otherwise it is not *the* game but *a* game), are, in the United States, discussed in constitutional terms, *i.e.* in legal terms that may have no meaning outside the United States.

Thus I have been very struck by the discussions over the agreements by the United States Government to have American soldiers stationed abroad tried for ordinary criminal offenses by the courts of the country where they are stationed. I may have missed it, but in any case I have not seen any mention of the fact that this is hardly a subject for discussion and decision solely in the Congress of the United States. For if no agreement is made, I know of no principle that enables the Congress to legislate so as to deprive British courts of their normal jurisdiction in Britain over any American soldiers, if such there be, as are charged with offenses against the British civil law. It may be that the Declaration of Independence has been repealed in reverse. If this is so, the fact ought to be announced to a candid and astonished world.

An American representative, carrying out the will of Congress, might say to Britain that only if it waives jurisdiction will American airmen be stationed there. But the bargain, if there is to be one, is not capable of simple decision by indignant congressmen whose innocent voters have been turned over to the infamous courts of Queen Elizabeth II, sent to prisons without television sets in the cells, and otherwise deprived of their inalienable rights. That Americans abroad have to take their luck—have to run the risk of not getting all the safeguards of their own unparalleled legal system—is one of the facts of life concealed from politicians so deeply soaked in their own tradition that they cannot realize that it is not of universal and automatic applicability.

Innocently enough, what these statesmen are arguing for

is the acceptance, by powers as different as Britain and Iceland, of a system of "capitulations," involving a preferential system of courts as was imposed on China, Japan, Turkey, and Egypt in the old and odious days of imperialism. I think a reversion to the outmoded epoch of Palmerston—and Commodore Perry—is unlikely. To quote Chesterton on a slightly different case:

Ere every shop shall be a store,
And every trade, a trust,
    Lo! many men, in many lands, know when their cause is just.
There will be quite a large attendance,
When we declare our independence.

Difficulties Created by New Nations

So far I have spoken of nations with common aims, common traditions, common verbal formulas, but all that I have said applies, of course, far more seriously to nations that do not recognize a common aim, have no deep-rooted common traditions, have no common political language. And a fact that we have got to notice and allow for is that the number of these nations is much greater than it was even thirty years ago. The number of nations with whom, say, the United States has to get along somehow is not merely multiplied numerically, it is a multiplication of political societies whose indigenous political traditions are not those of the United States, Great Britain, or France, in which verbal similarities nearly always deceive, in which common formulas turn out on examination not to be common, and in which the common political language is at least as artificial as Esperanto.

It is important to contrast the present situation with that of England as seen by someone like Mr. Podsnap a century ago. I have chosen the comparison because the United States is, in many ways, the equivalent of England a century ago.

If you doubt this, look at an old volume of *Punch,* read the speeches of people like Roebuck in Parliament, read even acute and wise political writers like John Stuart Mill and Walter Bagehot. There is in them some of the widespread American belief that there is a known system of political, economic, and moral values that the world should and can copy, no doubt imperfectly, but nevertheless with universally beneficent effects. There is the same irritation at the refusal of the world to do this, or at the odd and unorthodox results of such efforts as are made. There is the same fact of general unpopularity, even if there are different national reactions to that fact.

But, and it is a very important "but," the English situation was much simpler, the problems more easily handled. First of all, leaving out the rather intangible force of national psychology, national conceit, national indifference to the opinion of outsiders, it was possible to believe that there were known and right, that is British, political solutions that the world could, and what was more would, adopt. An American today may have as innocent a faith in his political institutions as had Lord Tennyson, but he cannot have the same faith in their universal appeal. The folly or the sin of the world is brought home to the American by his newspaper, by television, his senators, and by the American Legion, to name only a few of the forces battering daily on the American psyche. Even if the naive explanation of treason is adopted to account for the deplorable state of the world, the fruits of treason are there.

For the Englishman, it was a more hopeful world. Over a considerable part of it, let us be frank and say "the white world," right—that is, English—institutions could be exported. Jeremy Bentham believed in the vendibility of his constitutional nostrums in Latin America. For Henry Hallam, the discovery of representative government, by which he meant the English parliamentary system, was an invention of the same importance and magnitude as the steam engine. It might be, and the more pessimistic John Stuart Mill believed that it was, too much to expect that all the world could accept English political institutions. The best that India could hope for was another Akbar, another Charlemagne or the Honourable the East India Company—a collective Akbar. But in India, in China, and later in Africa, if the whole political system could not be exported, the essentials could be—law, order, the limited liability company, and with them their material products, the steamer, the locomotive, and the power loom with their beneficent results in annihilating distance, promoting unity, and elevating the level of existence of the peoples who had not invented either Magna Carta or the separate condenser. Adam Smith had seen human history, so Bagehot declared, as the progress of the mass of mankind to the dignity of Scotchmen. For Scotchmen you could read Englishmen, Frenchmen, or Americans if mere national vanity forced the modification of Professor Smith's self-evident truth.

In such a situation, some of the problems that most concern us did not exist or were swept under the carpet for us to deal with in our time. The spread of representative government, of the common law or of the Code Napoléon were necessary conditions of progress, but conditions fairly easily fulfilled. And where they were not fulfilled spontaneously or where they were not "received," as the Roman law was, in some of the more enlightened countries of Europe in the sixteenth century—France, the Netherlands, Scotland—the minimum conditions of progressive and civilized political living could be imposed. The whole world could be remade as the Mediterranean and the West European world had been remade by the Romans, and every expanding European nation plus the United States thus quoted Virgil to its own satisfaction, "hae nobis erunt artes."

A very good, and for our modern world a most important,

example is furnished by the spirit of British rule in India as exemplified in the role of Macaulay. Macaulay had both long-term, intelligent views and short-term, short-sighted views. He believed that if certain institutions were imported and, if necessary, imposed, certain beneficent results would follow whether the peoples of India wanted them or not. All just government might derive its powers from the consent of the governed, although Macaulay did not believe this self-evident truth, but good government need not do so. So Macaulay did not wait till the devotees of Kali, vulgarly known as the Thugs, renounced their murderous beliefs; he legislated against them, making lavish use of the convenient principle of "guilt by association." He and Lord William Bentinck did not wait until orthodox Hinduism renounced suttee. They legislated vigorously against it. Macaulay had no doubt that English culture was superior to Indian culture, and he would, I fear, have had no doubts even if he had known anything about Indian culture. In India he was not an Oxford romantic, but a Cambridge rationalist.

More important, Macaulay consciously imported English law and the English language into India to weaken the old Hindu culture and to make possible the creation of a body politic based on sound, *i.e.* on English, foundations. When that time came, English rule would have justified and ended itself. Here Macaulay was both a prophet and blind. For he foresaw, correctly, the rise of Nehru and the inevitable results of the rise of Nehru, but not the rise of Gandhi or the creation of Pakistan. But modern India is, in great part, a creation of men who did believe that political and social institutions could be exported and imposed, who did not believe that the customer is always right, and who behaved more like an old-fashioned parent making the child eat its spinach, than a modern parent afraid of breeding resentments and psychoses.

I have dwelt a little on this parallel because I think it does bring out the especial difficulty of our situation today. No one, not even the English, believe in the universal exportability or imposability of even our best political and social institutions. And far from finding a world in which there is agreement among the nations that count about what is the good political and social life, we find the world divided between two great and competing systems, each confronted by sales resistance from the uncommitted nascent nations, which are, in turn, united on only one thing—they will neither be led nor driven. They must be coaxed to eat their spinach and they may, and often do, refuse to touch the stuff. They may prefer a totally different diet offered by a rival firm with quite as great access as we have to the media and sales devices of political advertising.

Rival Institutions and Competing Systems

In the nineteenth and early twentieth centuries, the Western European, or North Atlantic, world had no serious rivals. If China or India or the Islamic world awoke from its dogmatic slumber, we could assume that they would turn to us. Today we cannot assume anything of the kind. They may turn to a rival set of institutions, which, even when they use our words, mean very different things.

I do not propose to waste your time in arguing the point that Soviet communism, in its Russian or Chinese version, is different from and opposed to most of our basic political concepts. I know nothing about the internal politics of Communist Russia or Communist China, but circumstantial evidence is pretty decisive, as "when you find a trout in the milk" to quote Thoreau. Marxism or Marxism-Leninism is a European export, but it is at best a European heresy. We do not need, I hope, to argue with ourselves the point that the political vocabulary of the Soviet bloc, so far as it flatters ours by imitation, flatters only to deceive. Here what causes endless friction is not a mere difference in institutions and vocabulary but in purpose. One society expects, wishes, and works for the death of the other.

There are many things we ought to know about international communism and about the political structure of the Communist states, but for my topic it suffices to know this. It is not in the areas directly subjected to Communist rule in the two great Communist states that the institutional differences are important. It is in the penumbra, in nations like Poland, forcibly subdued by Communism, and in nations on the edge of the Communist world state that are, whether they know it or not, threatened by it. It is there that institutional differences, verbal differences, variations in the political attitudes behind the verbal and institutional differences are important and give room both for hope and fear.

In these areas, in Europe at any rate, I think that there is more reason for hope than fear, but I must admit that people who know these countries much better than I do are not always so confident. I have known intelligent Germans who think that it is far from impossible that the Communists may have reared a Communist-minded population in East Germany, and I have known Poles who express the same fears about Poland. Whether at the present moment, while the game of musical chairs is being played for keeps in the satellites, these observers are still so fearful, I cannot say. But even if the impression of monolithic and victorious government has been destroyed by the Soviet leaders, it does not follow that all the educational work of those leaders has been made futile. The transformation of our common political vocabulary has had some results. Certain simple political dogmas widely held in the United States, for instance, are not now—if they ever were—held in these enslaved countries. I cannot think that any ideological importance will be attached to the question whether the solution of Washington's transport system may involve creeping socialism will matter in Warsaw or in the politics of a piccolo player in East Berlin. These may be burning questions in Buncombe County, but people in Eastern Europe have more serious things to think about. If "freedom" means a passionate devotion to *laissez faire,* it is not a word to stir men to take great risks in these unhappy lands.

Freedom has a great emotive power, and in Eastern Europe it has very much the emotive power it has in our countries; although the Communist may have aimed in the satellite states at creating "cities without memory," they have not yet succeeded. But the term "freedom" is ambiguous. It may mean simply "national" freedom, and that may mean tangible territorial organization rather than a body of ethical principles embodied in political institutions. There are, I am certain, millions of Poles for whom the Polish possession of Breslau or Wroclaw takes primacy over "freedom" in the political sense, and there are millions of Germans for whom the unity of Germany (including Wroclaw or Breslau) takes precedence over the needs of the North Atlantic Treaty Organization.

But it is when we turn to the new nations that the difficulties become overwhelming.

There is a sense in which all the ideas moving the world today are of European or North Atlantic origin, for what Sir Henry Maine said of the Greeks is truer of us. The moving forces, ideological and technological, that are changing darkest Africa and the heart of Asia, come from us. Marx and the bulldozer, the Rights of Man and the atom bomb, all are our inventions. It is easy—and hopeful—to note that indisputable fact and to conclude from it that we are, as the nineteenth century liberals thought, all moving toward the adoption of a political religion of all sensible men. But there are two things to be borne in mind before we come to that conclusion.

There are at least two versions of the European world view on the market, one of which is the sworn enemy of the other.

That we find it easy enough to accept. Communism is the enemy. The Communist use of words like "freedom," "democracy," "republic," and "equality" is bogus so we confidently and, in general rightly, assume. But we are inclined to forget that this assumption is *ours,* not that of the new nations to whom the two rival recipes for the good, the free, the democratic life are being offered. We cannot be sure that we have the goods that, with proper advertising, will get people to beat a path to our door. It is not only that the best mouse trap does not always attract the customers—advertising is needed—but it is also not certain that this section of humanity wants mousetraps. It may want mice.

A parallel in the field of religion may cast some light. More than forty years ago, it was possible for great missionary congresses to plan for the Christianizing of the world in a generation. Do any dare plan that way today? In the case of China, the Communist government may be effectively stifling the seed so hopefully planted. And in Africa, Islam is making more progress than Christianity, not because we need think it better, but because it is more suited to the immediate needs of a primitive society. Without pushing the parallel too far, we may take warning that the good cause does not win solely in virtue of its goodness; it has to be adapted to its new and hostile or indifferent environment.

Secondly, the rival creed may take over our slogans and give them new and plausible institutional forms. Here is the reverse of the comforting belief that our doctrines alone move the world. Because this is so, words and things from our arsenal have a high prestige value. But the words and things that we offer may be not quite the words or things that are wanted. They may be too complicated and too expensive, as Christianity is a complicated and expensive religious system compared with Islam. By freedom, liberty, democracy, and self-government, we mean a lot of linked—but not identical—institutions, not all formally political. We mean a free press, free television, free trade unions, religious free-dom, and a legal system that respects the individual more than the state purpose. All of these hang together, and it is doubtful that they can survive separately. But the words, transformed by sophistry, can survive and flourish, and al-though they are our words, they do not stand for our things.

Thus "democracy" in Asia may not be a series of social and political institutions that give a high value to the individual. The Communists may give it, or appear to give it, to the Asian masses in forms that, to our minds, completely trans-form and destroy the values that we call democratic. We underestimate, I think, the degree to which this transforma-tion can be carried out, and the word successfully transferred from our camp to theirs. As I said much earlier, "democracy" is a vaguer, a more emotion charged word and a more emo-tive word than "republic," and it is susceptible of more manipulation. We have to face the fact that "democratic in-stitutions" may plausibly mean what we call tyranny and that if we think always in our own terms and never pause to consider what the words can be made to mean, if we think that they are identical and must necessarily appear identical with the principles of the American or British constitutions, our political warfare for the minds and adherence of the new nations will not win many battles in Asia, whatever it may do on Capitol Hill.

More important is the ambiguity of the word "freedom." It is not the same as "liberté" or as "Freiheit," but it is still less the same as "Merdeka." In countries where the problem of nationalism was solved, one way or another, a long time ago, liberty can mean a great many things *including* national freedom from foreign domination. In countries newly emerg-ing to national status, it overwhelmingly, often exclusively, means freedom from foreign government even from a for-eign government providing more of the other meanings of freedom than the emergent national government seems likely to do. For the nationalist that does not matter. "Liberté, liberté chérie" as the "Marseillaise" puts it, means merely that impure foreign blood is to be soaked up by the freed land. To that end, all other meanings of freedom are cheerfully sacrificed.

It is not my place, here, to discuss whether this shows an intelligent sense of values. I accept it as a political fact of the world we live in. It is important to do that, and it is also important not to think that "freedom," in this sense, necessarily means freedom in any other sense. It is because it may not mean freedom in any other sense that minorities in nations "rightly struggling to be free" try to invent—and sometimes succeed in inventing—a new nationality, or at any rate succeed in contracting out of the national freedom of the bigger group. Thus the rise of Magyar nationalism produced Croat nationalism, and the triumph of Irish and Indian nationalism produced Northern Ireland and Pakistan. People who do not feel that throwing off one particular form of foreign yoke is all that matters naturally balk at sacrificing everything else to that end. But, in general, we may take it that national freedom, once the question is on the tapis, is the terminus to which all active political movements tend. For good or ill, this is how the world wags.

It does not follow, however, that we know anything more of a "freed" nation than that it is "freed" in this sense. I think it is a common American error to conclude that it does. It may not come to care for our other freedoms at once or, given our short life span, in any time that concerns us. We may believe that peoples are bound to come to want our freedom, but when, in what long run? In the long run we shall all be dead, as Keynes said. We cannot assume that the new nations will automatically share our prepossessions, or that if they use our words, as well they may, they will use them in our sense. We must not be surprised when a new nation that we think owes us a good deal is not only ungrateful ("ungratitude more strong than traitor's arms" is a national fault of all nations), but definitely blind to their own necessities and interests.

First of all, by that we may mean our necessities and interests, and we may mean this innocently. We may see the outside world in terms of our natural priorities and expect all nations to see things that way. This is not peculiarly a fault of any one nation. The possible collapse of the French position in North Africa is at the moment, for example, much more a preoccupation of the French people than their duty to NATO or the Russian menace. This may be wrong, but when I read the accounts of the recent Minnesota primary carefully, I did not see much to show that problems of foreign policy were much in the minds of the voters of that highly literate and intelligent state.

It is absurd to expect that a nation still shaky on its feet, still suffering from the birth trauma, will be constantly preoccupied with the same questions as the Department of State or even the Foreign Office. And we can be quite certain that, as will be brought home to you later in this series, the new nations of Asia will not see the recent story of their liberation in our terms. They will, if they permit themselves the luxury of private candor, know that their chief liberator, in the sense of destroying the material and psychological basis of white empire, was not the United States but Japan. Some of the leaders of these new nations would have to have very bad memories not to remember this, and some, it is a fact to be faced, will think that another liberating force is or was Communist China. They will not see the "Communist menace" in our terms, if they see it at all. And if they see it at all, they will react against it in their own terms.

We have had a neglected example of that in recent weeks in Indonesia. It has been the strength of orthodox Islam that has reduced, or possibly removed, Communist power from the central government of Indonesia. To Islam, however, the sacred American doctrine of the separation of church and state is not so much wrong as unintelligible. So it would have been, for very different reasons, to an Athenian or a Roman who gave us so much of our political vocabulary.

Americans are right to congratulate themselves on their success in helping to create a free nation in the Philippines, in avoiding the mistakes and greeds of imperialism on the British and French models. The founders of the Philippine colony of the United States had not necessarily such elevated notions; they saw Manila as another Hong Kong, and if that dream had proved practicable, there might, I only say *might,* have been a stronger imperialist party in the United States.

I am very ready to admit that American pride is justified. But Americans were lucky in that they made their experiment in imperialism, or liberation, in the only Christian country in the Orient, where a great many of the ways of thought and habits of political organization were deeply embedded before Admiral Dewey sailed into Manila Bay. If all the Filipinos had been Moros, the story might have been different, just as if all the Indonesians and not merely the Amboynese had been Christianized, instead of being the last great conquest of Islam, the history of Indonesia would have been different and its political problems today not necessarily easier, but more intelligible.

I do not wish to insinuate that effective kindred political institutions can only be set up by new nations that are Christian. They may be set up by countries that have developed their own effective and "modernizable" political institutions and have developed for example, their own effective, modern-minded middle class. The Japanese had invented the department store long before they adapted, with real if limited success, so many European institutions; the two facts are not, I think, disconnected. It was not for nothing that a generation ago they were known as "the British of the Far East," which, at that time, was a boost not a knock.

It is of great interest that a member of the Supreme Court of the United States has been able to discuss together the working of the court systems in the United States and in India. Justice Douglas has been able to do this because Macaulay, Maine, and James Fitzjames Stephen gave British India British legal institutions. There was no Indian demand for the principles of the common law or of an independent judiciary, any more than there was a demand for parliamentary government, which has taken root so quickly. It would be absurd to expect the Indians to be grateful for this, although some are. They were put into a reform school against their will and cannot be expected to like their teachers, but it is possibly permissible to notice that the reform school did produce some reform, which is more than can be said for most reform schools.

All that I am trying to suggest, in a somewhat reckless canter over a vast area, is that we cannot take for granted the survival value of our political institutions in a continent where they have never been known at all, or have been known as foreign and so unpopular importations; that many new nations have been projected on to the stage of history, less by their own actions, than by the vicissitudes of world politics; and that the old nineteenth century idea that our institutions were inevitably destined to conquer by their excellence is as vain as the belief that Asia in this century would become Christian.

What are we to make of the rather depressing situation that I have described?

First of all, we should clear our minds of cant or of false hopes. Whatever we do, we shall be—that is our leaders will be—in the position of Marshal Foch, not of Napoleon or of Stalin. The main, though not the exclusive, interest uniting the NATO powers, for instance, is the preservation of their national autonomy. As for the neutrals, the uncommitted, this is, as I have suggested, often the only political interest that they have in common with us. We must get along with some diversity of command and some difference in timing. At any given moment, some independent nations, not in the the Communist camp, will be more conscious of what binds them to others in the same situation, others will be less conscious. In free societies, only obvious, acutal, and frightening danger can abolish, for the moment, local priorities. We may all want freedom, democracy, justice, but not all will want them in the same way and at the same time. So we learn little by hearing that we all want these things, if we do not break down this statement into more concrete terms, find out what these words mean in the given social and political context and what they mean, in order of priority, at this moment.

This being so, we must be ready to accept anomalies and weaknesses, what we call bad national habits in our allies, friends, or non-enemies. Thus it is a practically universal British belief that the American party system needs fundamental reform, that it should be made rational and efficient, that is, British. I have spent many years trying to convince my countrymen that this is not so, that the last thing we should want is a rational American party system, and that if we are foolish enough to want it, we shall not get it.

In the same way, continental critics who want the British to define the Commonwealth ask for a vain thing. Were it defined, it might vanish. Americans who want to give to "freedom" all the overtones of what is called the "free enterprise system" will find that they are practically alone in that desire.

We shall have to accept the possibility that new nations who have not grown up in our traditions, although they may have grown up under their shadow, are unlikely, spontaneously, to reproduce effective working models of the British or the American constitutions. They have many new problems to solve; we must be prepared for the possibility that they will solve them in new ways, ways that may seem odd to us. If they do not also seem dangerous, we should be content. We are living on borrowed time in Asia and Africa, and speed—with all the risks of disaster—is safer than delay with the certainty.

This should not breed in us an inferiority complex, an apologetic attitude. We should be prepared to point out to the new nations that unlike St. Paul, we bought our freedom at a great price and that the best things in life are not free. No new nation will reach a modern standard of well-being and power without intense self-examination. We do new nations no good by letting them blame everything in their condition on ill luck. In nations, as in individuals, luck is often character. But within that limiting consideration, we should be ready to see kindred aims in different institutions.

We should not deny the importance of politics. The Soviet Union is proving that importance at this moment. The gilt is being stripped from that ginger bread. We can emphasize this, point out, tactfully, that institutions that permit the rule of Stalin are bad, and call the Soviet witnesses to prove our point.

Finally, we should not forget that all political devices, in our tradition, have one justification—the well being and the dignity of the individual. All schemes that turn out to sacrifice him to the mass turn out to sacrifice him to a group of individuals, all of them scoundrels as they candidly point out. We must put up with and adjust to real divergencies in means and not in ends. For the ends will to some extent control the means, but if we think solely of means, and lay down absolute rules of political progress, we shall lose allies and fail to win friends. The very human diversity of the political societies we have to deal with is part of our tradition, part of what we treasure. We may continuously feel and think of a pattern laid up in heaven, but we should beware of thinking that it has been embodied on earth, in the United States or Scotland.

4

Emerging Requirements for an Expanding World Economy

EDWARD S. MASON[1]

"EMERGING" is a pliable word. Its geologic meaning may cover a few thousand years. Fruit flies, on the other hand, emerge quickly. What does it mean in terms of the problems with which political economy may be expected to deal? A period of the order of ten to twenty years and certainly not more than a quarter century is what I suspect the genial entrepreneur of this lecture series had in mind. Beyond twenty-five years—and certainly beyond fifty—the future belongs to biology and technology.

We appear in various large, heavily populated areas of the world to be on the verge of changes in the rate of population growth that, within a relatively short period of time, may convert figures of 1 to 1.5 per cent per annum into figures of 2 to 3 per cent. At a 3 per cent rate, population doubles every twenty-five years and not much more than three centuries would be needed to supply the world with a person for every square yard of standing room. No kind of "economizing of scarce resources" using existing technologies can cope with this kind of problem. On the other hand, if science can unsalt the seas and water deserts, produce energy by fission and fusion from limitless sources of fissionable materials, release the nutrient possibilities of marine vegetation, and unlock the resources of new planets, perhaps man's apparently irresistable impulse to reproduce himself can be accommodated. But these are vistas and solutions with which an economist can rightfully have no truck.

[1] Dean, Graduate School of Public Administration, Harvard University.

Our problem is to consider what rearrangements of re-sources use are economically practicable and politically feasible and may be expected to assist an expanding world economy within the limits of known and foreseeable technology, and in relation to a number of people and a set of wants that are not too different from those currently existing. Within a ten- to twenty-year period, it is possible to surmise that the economic problems now confronting us are not going to be altered out of recognition either by a population explosion or a technological revolution. But though we may call these problems economic, it is well to recognize at the outset that we are operating in the realm of political economy. The obstacles to world economic growth arise very largely from the power drives of various national states and from the domestic struggles for preferment of various pressure groups. A renewal or lessening of these obstacles calls more for the talents of the politician than those of the economist. One final caveat—our subject, by its definition, demands extensive rather than intensive cultivation. Let those who seek a well-rounded and penetrating treatment of, say, convertibility follow their interests elsewhere.

Production Versus Trade

Our subject concerns requirements for an expanding world economy. Note that the emphasis is on production rather than trade. But can world output grow without a commensu-rate growth in world trade? The historical answer appears to be a qualified "yes," at least for very large areas, but the facts suggest that during periods when trade was growing less rapidly than output the rate of increase in output was low. If the output of the non-Soviet world is to grow rapidly during the next quarter century, there appear strong reasons for believing that international trade must grow at least as fast as output. And if both output and trade are to grow together, there must be not only a balanced expansion in the production of foodstuffs, raw materials, energy sources, and manufactures but also an expansion in those geographical areas that facilitate international exchange. We are concerned in this lecture with some of the difficulties that appear to confront a balanced expansion in the "proper" geographical areas and with the trade and other policies to which we might look to overcome these difficulties.

Glancing backward for a moment, it is interesting to note the striking difference between the relation of economic growth to foreign trade in the United States and Russia as against the rest of the world. From 1900 on, exports and imports have been a small and declining percentage of the national income of the United States. Foreign trade constituted an even smaller percentage of the national income of Russia, and since the emergence of the Union of Soviet Socialist Republics, it has dwindled to insignificant figures. For the rest of the world, on the other hand, foreign trade has constituted a much higher percentage of total output, and from 1870 to the onset of the great depression the rate of growth of foreign trade was as high as, or somewhat higher than, the rate of growth in total output. During the 1930's, of course, even excluding the United States and the Soviet Union, the established relation between world output and trade was broken. But since the end of the war, the figures, excluding the Soviet bloc, indicate a rate of growth in trade that has exceeded the rate of growth in world output.[2]

The expansion of the trade of the Soviet Union with

[2] This discussion of relationships between world trade and world output relies heavily on the following sources: League of Nations, *Industrialization and Foreign Trade*, (1945); W. A. Lewis, "World Production, Prices and Trade, 1870-1960," XX The Manchester School 105 (May 1952); and W. A. Lewis, *Theory of Economic Growth* (1955), Chap. VI; various staff publications of the Contracting Parties to the General Agreement on Tariffs and Trade, in particular, *International Trade* (1952).

its satellites probably indicates a substantial modification of the traditional policy of self-sufficiency of the Soviet Union, but I do not believe that during the period under consideration, we are likely to see any considerable growth of what has come to be called East-West trade. The reasons have to do mainly with the lack of any serious degree of economic dependence of the Soviet bloc on outside sources, with the greater ease of fitting domestic production with the requirements of a planned economy, and with the inherent difficulties of establishing stable and calculable trade relationships between state trading and non-state trading countries. To hold this view is not to assert that the Soviet Union or China will refrain from undertaking trade agreements for political as well as economic reasons or that Soviet ventures into foreign lending will not have trade repercussions. These are questions that I shall return to presently. The possibilities of a sizable East-West trade seem to me slight, but rather than attempting adequately to justify this view, let us assume what might have to be proved in order to get back to our central theme of the relationship of trade to output in the non-Soviet world.

The United States, contrary to the experience of the rest of the non-Soviet world, has for the last half century seen a decline in the ratio of foreign trade to output. There are, however, some fairly strong reasons for believing this trend may be reversed. They have, of course, to do with the prospects of an increasing dependence of the United States on imported foodstuffs and raw materials and with the persistence of aid programs in our foreign policy.

The President's Materials Policy Commission, reporting in 1952, estimated that by 1975 this country would be importing 20 per cent of its requirements for foodstuffs and raw materials as against a current figure of 9 per cent. In 1952 the median census estimate of the rate of population growth yielded a figure of 193 millions for 1975, which was used by the commission in making its projections. Since then the

median census estimate has been revised upward to 210 millions, which represents nearly a 10 per cent increase. If per-
capita production is not adversely affected by this projected
increase in the rate of population growth—and there is no
reason to suppose it will be—this means approximately a 10
per cent increase in raw material requirements and perhaps
a still larger increase in the share of imports. These estimates
of course assume an expansibility of output of foodstuffs and
raw materials in foreign areas and trade barriers no higher
than at present. If these assumptions are not fulfilled and this
country has to depend more extensively on domestic sources,
the result—as I have argued elsewhere—might be a moderate, but not a large, check to our rate of economic growth.[3]
The economic expansion of the United States, at least over
the next one or two decades, is relatively invulnerable to
adverse influences on foreign sources of supply. But the
United States is about the only nation in the non-Soviet world
of whom this can be said.

The main point, however, is that with anything approaching favorable trade policies and conditions of production
abroad, the ratio of foreign to domestic production in the
United States, which has been steadily downward for the last
fifty years, is likely to be reversed. There are, furthermore,
other reasons for believing that rapid growth of output in the
non-Soviet world must be accompanied by an increasing ratio
of trade to total output. Many large underdeveloped areas
of the world have tended to stagnate at very low levels of
foreign trade. The ratio of Indian imports to national income,
for example, has recently averaged about 7 per cent. But
both experience of the nineteenth century and an analysis
of current requirements for growth in underdeveloped areas
suggest that economic expansion is likely to be accompanied
by an increasing ratio of foreign trade to domestic output.

[3] E. S. Mason, "American Security and Access to Raw Materials,"
World Politics (January 1949); E. S. Mason, "Raw Materials, Rearmament and Economic Development," *Quarterly Journal of Economics* (May
1952).

The foreign exchange requirements for economic growth in most underdeveloped countries are very large regardless of the direction of economic development. Even agricultural expansion in Southern Asia, involving as it does the need to bring new acres under cultivation by irrigation and drainage schemes, is likely to have a sizable foreign exchange component. And for industrialization, the foreign exchange component is very high. In Pakistan, for example, railway investment over-all has a foreign exchange requirement of over 50 per cent of the net investment, and investment in the current public power and irrigation program has a foreign exchange component of over 30 per cent.

What this means is that if economic growth is to be rapid in many large underdeveloped areas of the world, the growth of foreign trade will have to be even more rapid. The foreign exchange requirements for growth can be earned by increased exports or met by capital imports. In either case, though not to the same degree, an expansion of foreign trade is indicated.

Finally, although there is little reason to believe that the foreign trade of Western Europe will regain the relationship to European output that existed before 1930, there is good reason to believe that the *rate of growth* of foreign trade will remain high. The great depression fastened on most of the industrial countries of the world a system of agricultural protection that appears likely to be one of the most enduring institutions of our time. This, coupled with the excessive protection to manufacturers in many primary producing countries, results in a fundamental distortion of the geographical division of labor that appears to preclude, for a long time to come, a re-establishment of pre-1930 relationships between world trade and world production. But the rate of increase in trade since the war has been somewhat greater than the rate of increase in output, and there are strong reasons for believing that if world output grows rapidly, world trade will also grow rapidly.

One cautionary remark, however, seems in order before we turn to a consideration of some of the difficulties confronting us in obtaining balanced growth in the non-Soviet world. It seems possible that a sizable increase in output in the non-Soviet world—even in per-capita output—may be realized over the next fifteen to twenty years even with a declining ratio of trade to output. The technical potentialities of substituting domestic for foreign output are sufficiently great, particularly in countries well endowed in natural resources, to make it unwise to rule out this possibility. It seems clear, however, that even in the economically least vulnerable countries, a failure of foreign sources of supply to grow will constitute a substantial check to economic expansion, and over most of the non-Soviet world, it appears probable that an expansion of trade at a somewhat greater rate than output is a necessary condition to rapid growth.

The Notion of Balanced Growth

If world production and trade are to grow rapidly, there must be a balanced expansion of raw materials, foodstuffs, energy sources, and manufactures, and their expansion must occur in the right geographical areas. To say that the essential components of economic growth must be in balance is, of course, as platitudinous as to say that the external payments position of a country must be in balance. But payments can balance at a high or low level of trade and so also can the relationship among the various components of economic growth balance at low or high rates of growth. It makes a lot of difference to the over-all rate of growth—though not to the maintenance of balance among the components—whether the expansion of output in various of these components encounters serious technological or institutional difficulties.

The maintenance of a balanced rate of growth obviously

does not mean that outputs of raw materials, foodstuffs, energy materials, and manufactures have to move at the same rate. There is a strong tendency for inputs of raw materials per dollar of finished products to decline over time as these materials are subject to greater degrees of processing. The use of energy materials in terms of heat units has grown somewhat more slowly than aggregate output in Western Europe and at about the same rate as output in the United States. The requirements for energy materials would quite clearly have increased at a much faster rate in the absence of phenomenal increases in efficiency in energy conversion and use. The world production of foodstuffs in real values tends to increase more slowly than raw materials or energy outputs and much more slowly than manufactures. During the period 1880 to 1930, world production of manufactures grew at an average annual rate of about 4 per cent; raw materials at about 3.5 per cent; foodstuffs at 2 per cent; and energy inputs at a little over 3 per cent.

The optimum relationship among these rates with respect to over-all growth will obviously depend on what consumers —and increasingly governments—want in the way of finished products and on technological changes affecting the relative costs of producing different types of output. But given these ultimate consumption requirements and technical possibilities, there is some relationship among rates of expansion of these large components that is optimum with respect to aggregate growth. A failure of certain components to grow would, of course, increase the relative price of these components, and this price increase would induce substitution. There are large possibilities of substitution among energy materials, foodstuffs, and other raw materials. There are even unlimited possibilities of using traditional foodstuffs for energy conversion and traditional industrial raw materials as foodstuffs. But the substitution possibilities among these large components are marginal. In general we have to have energy materials in the right quantities and raw materials in the right quantities if aggregate output is to expand. The failure of some large source of customary supply of any of these —say Middle Eastern oil—can have most serious consequences on aggregate output.

If an increase in the relative price of some important component is the inevitable result of physical scarcities, there is little that institutional rearrangement or changes in public policy can do about it. There is, however, enough information regarding grades and quantities of mineral deposits, available energy resources, and the potential productivity of agricultural lands to justify a judgment that, over the next fifteen to twenty years, even assuming a rapid rate of population growth, there are no technical reasons that an adequate expansion of the various components of economic growth cannot take place without substantial increases in real costs. If growth potential is to be checked, it will be primarily the result of actions taken by governments.

It is not enough, however, that adequate expansion of the various components of growth takes place somewhere and somehow. If the requirements of various countries dependent on external supplies are to be met, these supplies must be available in areas that can provide adequate markets for imports. It is not sufficient that North America produces large volumes of exportable wheat and cotton if the rest of the world cannot earn the dollar exchange necessary to meet their cotton and wheat requirements from American sources. Nor can Japan meet its import requirements unless these imports are available from areas in which it has a competitive advantage over other potential suppliers.

At this point the question will be asked: Why cannot the expansion of components necessary to economic growth be left to the unimpeded working of the price system? The answer is that a large part of it can and that the whole problem could be solved by the right kind of a price system. This statement, however, would have to be qualified by the recognition that in various large areas of the world an effective working of a price system implies changes in values, incentives, and institutions that could only come about through a long process of cultural change. The fact of the matter is that in many areas the right kind of a price system—with its implication of free international movement of goods and factors—is not going to be allowed to work. We have already noted the serious distortion in the international division of labor that has emerged from depression and war, resulting from the high degree of protection given agricultural production in industrialized countries and the high degree of protection given manufacturers in primary producing countries. This distortion, which arises from a very substantial interference with the working of the price system, is no doubt going to continue. There are, moreover, other interferences arising out of the full employment policies of various Western countries, and private and public wage and price controls, and other sources. To say that an international division of labor and a flow of goods and services in world trade conducive to expansion of aggregate output would take place if trade barriers were removed, price inflexibilities were eliminated, and monetary and fiscal policies were oriented toward external trade rather than toward domestic employment and welfare objectives, is not very helpful.

Any serious evaluation of the requirements for an expanding world economy must take as given certain national policies that interfere with the free movement of goods and services and consider how, within the limitations imposed by these policies, adverse impacts on economic growth can be minimized. At the same time, it must be recognized that in achieving a balanced expansion of the various components of economic growth, changes in relative prices perform a function for which there is no adequate substitute. More positive measures designed to remove structural imbalances or to assist the expansion of particular kinds of output in particular areas can at best supplement the profit opportunities registered by price relationships. What we have to consider, therefore, is how much of the job of facilitating an expansion of world output can and should be accomplished by pushing in the direction of trade and monetary policies to promote the international movement of goods and how much of the job will have to be accomplished by other means. Before examining this problem further let us take a look at the ways these questions have been tackled by United States foreign economic policy since the war and where we now stand.

United States Foreign Economic Policy Since the War

American foreign economic policy has, since the war, attempted two rather different gambits. The first, represented by the Bretton Woods institutions, later the General Agreement on Tariffs and Trade (GATT) and the Organization for Trade Cooperation (OTC) currently before Congress, has sought worldwide intergovernmental co-operation in promoting trade and payments arrangements designed to facilitate world trade. The second, illustrated by the Marshall Plan, the Point Four Program, and economic support for a number of military programs, has been designed to meet problems that were and are, for one reason or another, geographically limited. The relationships and interdependence among this international approach and these regional programs are interesting and justify comment.

A judgment on the success of the Bretton Woods approach can be harsh or lenient depending on how one assesses the extent of the obstacles overcome and on how the emphasis is distributed in describing the current situation. One dominating fact is that since the war world trade has recovered in remarkable fashion from the doldrums of the 1930's and has been growing at a somewhat faster rate than world output. In the course of this development, tariffs have been drastically scaled down, the European countries have largely abandoned quantitative restrictions, except for agricultural imports, and although exchange control machinery has not been dismantled, it is increasingly treated as standby capacity. The dollar and nondollar trading systems have been brought much closer together, and although complete current account convertibility keeps receding farther and farther into the distant future, discrimination against American exports is, in most parts of the trading world, not very serious. During the last few years, furthermore, exchange rates have been relatively stable, and finance ministers and central banks have shown signs of paying increasing attention to the importance of maintaining external stability by checking internal inflation. The contribution of Bretton Woods, including GATT, to all this has been decisive, and it must be said that a large step has been taken toward expanding that flow of goods in international trade on which an expanding world economy must increasingly depend.

If we look at the other side of the coin, however, the design makes a somewhat different impression. We are still a long way from that current-account-convertibility *cum* nondiscrimination that was the objective of the Bretton Woods enthusiasts, and since about 1953 progress has seemed increasingly difficult. The advance to date, moreover, has taken place under conditions of rising output and employment in the world in general and in the United States in particular, that are, or should have been, remarkably favorable to the reduction of trade barriers. The year 1956 nevertheless finds us in a situation where, because of inadequate currency reserves and other reasons, even a slight disturbance in the United States, or to a lesser degree elsewhere, could lead to a substantial setback in current trade and payments arrangements. Finally, the progress that has been made to date has been and continues to be vitally dependent on the willingness of the United States to supply the rest of the world $4 or $5 billion a year under special programs.

In these circumstances it would seem premature, to say the least, to consider the network of world trade substantially restored and to leave the "emerging requirements for an expanding world economy" exclusively to Bretton Woods and successor organizations. The fact of the matter is that the success of the internationalist strand of our foreign economic policy has been dependent to a large degree on the size and character of our regional programs, and this bids fair to be true over the period we are now surveying.

Before proceeding to a consideration of how these international and regional strands may be related to each other in the future, let us look for a moment at the character of our regional programs since the war. It was the expectation of the promulgators of Bretton Woods that the repairing of war damage and the correcting of economic dislocations in Europe would require a transition period before trade and payments arrangements would be able to get fully and effectively underway. The United Nations Relief and Rehabilitation Administration made a partial and inadequate contribution to the repair of war damage, and in 1947 when we were confronted by the political consequences of a failure of Western European recovery under the threat of Soviet encroachment and subversion, we embarked on the Marshall Plan. Although at first the Western European requirements were thought of exclusively in terms of balance-of-payments deficits, increasingly the problem came to be envisaged as an inadequate rate of economic growth to meet pressing claims for a higher standard of living and increasing defense requirements. But from its beginnings in a balance-of-payments analysis to its end as an adjunct to rearmament, the Marshall Plan was a regional program attempting to deal with the problems of an economically and politically related group of countries. Out of that program there developed a number of European organizations including the Organization for European Economic Cooperation and the European Payments Union that have persisted and may well continue indefinitely to have a function to perform.

Military programs are inevitably regional both for geographic and political reasons. The provision of dollars in United States military account has tended to center in Western European countries with their North African overseas territories; the Middle East, including Pakistan; and the Far East from Korea and Japan in the north to Vietnam and Thailand in the south. Since 1950 military purposes have absorbed an increasing percentage of the dollars supplied by foreign programs, and United States troop support and off-shore procurement have increasingly taken the place of out-right grants. In 1955 out of the nearly $3 billion supplied to Europe and North Africa, $840 million represented grants and the remainder off-shore procurement and troop support. Although these military expenditures have made no direct contribution to economic growth—in certain areas indeed growth has probably been handicapped—the dollars supplied have continued to meet balance-of-payments deficits, or what would have been deficits if Western Europe had not undertaken a drastic contraction of imports. A disappearance of this flow of dollars would certainly confront Western European countries with a difficult set of choices in adjusting their trade policies.

The current balance-of-payments positions of the Far Eastern countries receiving assistance from United States military programs are even more dependent on this flow of dollars than those of Western Europe. A cessation of this flow would force Japan, in particular, into drastic changes not only in the volume of its trade but its geographical orientation. Military assistance in the Middle East, including Pakistan, has a much larger component of equipment and supplies the provision of which does not yield dollars available for foreign spending. But these programs have frequently been accompanied by so-called defense support that has made a contribution to easing balance-of-payments difficulties. Taking United States military programs as a whole, it may be said that they are currently responsible in one way or another for the provision of about $4 billion a year. There can be little doubt that without this continued flow, the easing of trade barriers would have fallen substantially short of the position it has currently reached.

The third major regional element in our foreign economic policy has consisted of economic and technical assistance programs. These programs are, of course, regional only in the sense that the countries involved happen to be adjacent to each other. Not much in the way of regional organization has developed from assistance to underdeveloped areas, and it is questionable how much can or will. These programs may nevertheless properly be called regional as they are designed to deal with special problems that are common to groups of countries geographically related. If we exclude the Far Eastern programs as primarily concerned with defense support, the areas in which we are primarily interested are Latin America, the Middle East, and Southern Asia. Primarily for security reasons, our attention is increasingly focused on Southern Asia and the Middle East.

As we have seen, these regional programs have made a very large contribution to what measure of success has attended the internationalist strand of our foreign economic policy. But the reverse is also true. If it were not for the tremendous growth of foreign trade since the war, to which Bretton Woods has made a decisive contribution, the results of our attempts to bolster the economies of Western Europe, to improve the military potential of our allies, and to contribute to the economic development of underdeveloped areas would have been feeble indeed. Our problem now is to consider the respective roles of these and other aspects of our

foreign economic policy in meeting the emergency requirements for world economic growth over the next decade or
two.

Policy Alternatives

Currently, not only the foreign economic policy of the
United States but also the trading system of the non-Soviet
world seems to have reached something that might reason-
ably be called a plateau. There has been in recent years no
very striking further progress in the reduction of trade barriers, and although the purpose and geographical orientation
of the dollars supplied by United States foreign programs,
on which the whole system importantly depends, changes
perceptibly, the over-all magnitude remains remarkably constant. The chief efforts of the United States in the field of
foreign policy appear currently to be the attempts to persuade
Congress to legitimize the General Agreement on Tariffs
and Trade through approval of the proposed Organization
for Trade Cooperation, and to make provision for a continued flow of dollars into special foreign programs at about
the same rate as before. Despite heated charges that the proposed organization will subject the future of American business to the whims of foreigners and that continued expenditures abroad are the road to the poorhouse, to bankruptcy, or
worse, I doubt whether anyone, either in Congress or outside, is much excited by the foreign economic policy of this
country in the year 1956. The worst that can be said about
the program—and also the best—is that it is an unimaginative dishing up of more of the same.

There is not much reason that the trading system of the non-
Soviet world should not continue indefinitely on the present plateau if there is no sizable recession in the United
States; if inflationary movements in Britain and elsewhere
can be kept from getting out of hand; if the Soviet Union
does not too seriously disrupt the trading system through an

economic offensive; if the flow of Middle Eastern oil continues through present channels and on something like present terms; and if the United States does not disturb world commodity markets by injudicious disposal abroad of agricultural surpluses. If none of these unpleasant things happen, there is no particular reason that the trading system of the non-Soviet world should not continue to be a not intolerable and relatively stable mechanism. Of course this would mean that the rather sad lack of balance in the trade of Western Europe, Japan, and the rest of the world, now hidden by the flow of United States dollars, would continue to be hidden by their flow; that United States agricultural surpluses would continue to pile up with no place to go; and that the economies of the Middle East and Southern Asia would continue relatively stagnant at low levels of foreign trade. Nevertheless, it is some sort of a trading system, and its continued existence is not incompatible with economic growth in certain large areas of the free world.

Currently, the United States and its principal trading partners have open these alternatives: They can accept this system and live with it, trusting that when and if one or more of the serious potential disturbances that lurk around the corner heads into the open, *ad hoc* means can be found to deal with them. Or, they can attempt in advance to devise measures to manage contingencies that appear probable, and, over the longer run, prepare to move off the current plateau on to somewhat higher ground. In considering these alternatives, I recognize of course that there is a substantial gap between the task of criticizing current policy as unimaginative and suggesting measures that are not only imaginative but also workable.

Before attempting to discuss certain of the problems that appear to threaten the existing trading system, let me make the usual bow to various important but well-worn platitudes. Of course the United States has got to keep its depressions within the magnitude of 1949 or 1953 if a tightening of trade barriers is to be avoided. Of course the principal trading countries of the world, if they are to inflate, have got to keep their inflations in some sort of alignment if we are not to see an intensification of exchange restrictions. Furthermore, I would accept without reservation the prescription of the Economic Commission for Europe for a substantial expansion of European trade with the less developed areas of the world; to wit, a reduction of barriers against the importation of labor intensive products, including manufactured products, in the expectation that markets for the exports of capital intensive products will increase.[4] Let us assume that these developments occur. What important sources of trade disruption need further attention? Among others I should like to select for brief comment the question of Middle Eastern oil and the economic offensive of the Soviet Union in the Middle East and Southern Asia.

Most economically literate people are, I am sure, aware of the critical role that oil from the Middle East must play in the economic growth of the non-Soviet Eastern Hemisphere over the next fifteen to twenty years. In Europe something of the order of one half to three fourths of the projected increase in energy requirements within the time period we are considering must be met from this source, and there is no effective alternative supply. European coal production has about reached its peak, and efforts at expansion of annual outputs will yield little and that little at greatly increased costs. The sources of additional hydroelectric power are not large. In the light of the very rapid expansion of oil requirements in the Western Hemisphere, little help can be expected from the production of that area. A significant contribution of energy from atomic plants is still a decade or two off. Furthermore, what can be said about the dependence of the economic growth of

[4] U.N. Economic Commission for Europe, *Economic Survey of Europe in 1955* (1956).

Europe on Middle Eastern oil can also be said of most of Asia and Africa.

As everyone knows, the proved reserves of Middle Eastern oil are more than adequate to meet all possible requirements during the time period we are considering; the costs of extraction are low; and there are no technical transportation or conversion difficulties that need to be considered. Furthermore, at existing royalty rates the oil producing countries have now and in prospect all the capital and foreign exchange resources the most grandiose economic development plans for the area could require. Despite all this, it is obvious that this critical source of energy is in jeopardy, and the danger lies not only in the possibility of war but in the increasing tendency among various Arab states to use oil as a political weapon.

Although there are no technical difficulties in the transport of oil, pipe lines from Iraq and from the Persian Gulf cross the Arab states, and the Suez Canal, through which all westward tanker movements now proceed, has largely escaped from Western control. Furthermore, although the flow of oil may not be physically interrupted, there appears to be a growing disposition on the part of certain oil producing states to dictate to the companies the areas into which they will be allowed to ship. This is not only a desperate game for them to play but it is also a desperate game for us to allow to be played. The time has almost come for the United States Government to treat the problem of Middle Eastern oil as something more than a business matter to be handled by the oil companies with no other interposition—if I may use a Southern word—than prosecution under the antitrust laws. I do not pretend to know whether the antitrust laws have in fact been violated, but I must say that the current so-called cartel case seems to me to be magnificent in its irrelevance to any important interests the United States has in that part of the world.

If the Western countries with producing interests in the Middle East—which means mainly the United States, the United Kingdom, and France—and the companies themselves, are not to be whip-sawed, there must be some concert of action. The jointness of action seems almost more important than the kind of action taken. Furthermore, if we are to permit our foreign policy in that area to be in part determined by the oil companies, it is probably advisable to let them act together. On the whole, one foreign policy seems better than five. But although Mr. Berle has recently made an appealing case for allowing the companies to continue to make foreign policy, this is a proposition that most Americans will find it difficult to fit into an acceptable political philosophy, and I must confess it is difficult for me.[5] If concerted action has to be taken, I do not believe that it can be left to business interests no matter how well informed. To say more about a sensible handling of the problem of Middle Eastern oil requires more knowledge and more wisdom than I command. My only purpose is to call attention to a potentially critical impediment to a balanced expansion of the components of economic growth and one that is not going to be remedied by the working of the price system or any relaxation of barriers to trade.

Let us now turn briefly to the current so-called Soviet economic offensive and its possible impact on trade and economic growth in the non-Soviet world. The time has almost —but I assume not quite—arrived when one can talk sense about such subjects as East-West trade without being called a fellow traveler or worse. I propose to ride with what appears to be the trend and at least attempt to talk sense.

The issues that have come to the fore have to do with the possibilities of a serious disruption of commodity markets by a politically motivated Soviet purchase or sales campaign,

[5] A. A. Berle, Jr., *20th Century Capitalist Revolution* (1954), particularly Chap. IV.

the possible impact of an expansion of Soviet trade agreements, particularly with the countries of the Middle East and Southern Asia, and the significance of Soviet investments and offers to invest in developmental projects.

It is alleged that large state trading organizations operating without regard to profit and loss could seriously disrupt world commodity markets by either buying or selling operations. It is also charged that the possibilities of Soviet dumping of large stocks of strategic materials, such as tungsten, manganese, or antimony, currently discourages Western investment in the development of these materials. So far as the threat to the production of strategic materials is concerned, if it exists at all, it can certainly be easily countered by long-term purchase contracts, price guarantees, or other measures. The disruption of trading channels by politically motivated Soviet selling or buying is, no doubt, a theoretical possibility, but to date Soviet incursions into world markets are susceptible of other explanations. Of more important and immediate concern are actual, pending, and rumored trade agreements and investment programs.

If the primary producing countries of the Middle East and Southern Asia wish to enter into trade agreements with countries in the Soviet orbit, exchanging their cotton, jute, rubber, and rice for manufactured products, what interests of the non-Soviet world in general and the United States in particular are adversely affected? Presumably such trade would to some extent strengthen the Soviet world economically, but it is of the essence of trade that both sides benefit. The limiting factor to economic development in many of these countries is shortage of foreign exchange, and if inadequate foreign exchange earnings in the free world can be supplemented by imports of developmental goods from the Soviet orbit, the limits to economic growth may be to that extent removed. To be sure, if a primary producing country cannot find a market for its exports in the non-Soviet world and the Soviet Union uses its economic necessity as a pretext for demanding political concessions, both the country in question and the United States have reason to object. But, if the objection is to be effective, presumably some means have to be found either to expand, in the non-Soviet trading world, the markets for products of the country concerned or to supplement its foreign exchange receipts in some other way.

It would appear to me that if the central aim of Western policy in the Middle East and Southern Asia is to promote the political independence of the countries of the area and the growth of democratic processes so far as possible, and if the principal means comprise trade and aid related to economic development, then trade and aid from other than Western sources is not necessarily to be regarded as objectionable. Trade and aid from such sources are to be feared, of course, if they are used to extort political concessions, but the likelihood of this is great only if the countries concerned find themselves shut off from economic opportunities and assistance in the West. It is also to be feared if it handicaps rather than promotes economic developments, as it might well do if investment is encouraged in uneconomic directions. This possibility is real, and it raises questions concerning the conditions under which aid should be rendered and accepted, which I want to come back to presently.

Trade agreements between Southern Asian and Soviet countries lead, of course, to the exchange of trade delegations, and investment programs are accompanied by the movement of technical personnel. If it is feared that espionage and subversion will be thereby encouraged, it must be remembered that the Soviet Union can easily find other cover for their saboteurs, as recent activities in the Middle Eastern countries indicate. If it is feared that Soviet technical and administrative personnel will create favorable attitudes toward the Soviet Union because of their technical and administrative competence, this fear indeed may have some basis in fact.

But if the iron curtain between the Soviet orbit and the neighboring countries is going to have to be kept in place by our own efforts, I suspect these efforts are foredoomed to failure.

A cool assessment of the probable volume of East-West trade in Asia does not, I submit, favor any very sizable magnitudes. Indeed many countries both in Europe and Asia that have hopes of East-West trade development are likely to be sorely disappointed by the smallness of the opportunities. There is no country outside the Soviet orbit, with the possible exception of Afghanistan, whose trade with Soviet countries is more than a small fraction of its trade with the non-Soviet world, and the reasons this is likely to continue to be so are persuasive. Even Japan, whose prewar trade with countries now in the Soviet orbit was very large, is rapidly approaching a solution in which its foreign payments can be balanced at a satisfactory level without benefit of East-West trade.

Nor is it probable, I think, that Soviet capital assistance in underdeveloped areas will be very large for some time to come. To date this assistance has been more suggestion and rumor than fact. It is true that the investment in Afghanistan is real, but the steel mills for India and Pakistan and the Aswan dam for Egypt are still suggestions. Although Soviet assistance in investment is probably going to increase, it seems highly unlikely to me that it will rival Western investment in the Middle East or Southern Asia within the period we are discussing. What may happen, of course, is that the Soviet Union may concentrate capital and technical assistance in countries that are looking for political support against traditional enemies. This is true in the case of Afghanistan, and there appears to be no way for the West to avoid economic penetration by the Soviet Union short of espousing the Afghan cause against our own allies. Even so the problem in Afghanistan is not so much Soviet economic penetration as

political attitudes that are essentially independent of economic relations with the Soviet Union. The Egyptian-Czecho-
slovak cotton-for-arms deal presents a similar problem. There
was nothing within the compass of a sensible Western
foreign economic policy that could have prevented that deal.

The central point I am attempting to make is that so long
as trade agreements with the Soviet orbit and capital and
technical assistance from the Soviet Union promote economic
development in the Middle East and in Southern Asia—as
they may well do—there would appear to be little cause for
alarm. If the Soviet Union is able to wrest political concessions because these countries have nowhere else to turn for
markets or supplies, this is a failure of United States foreign
economic policy that we might correct. If these countries
accept aid from the Soviet Union as a part of a political
alignment they hope will serve their purposes against neighbors or against the West, it may represent a failure of Western policy but not necessarily of economic policy.

Before bringing to a conclusion this discussion of emerg-
ing requirements of an expanding world economy, let me
summarize the course of the argument to this point.

1. A rapid expansion of world output is likely to require
over the next decade or two an expansion of world trade at
about the same rate.

2. A balanced growth of output of manufactures, raw
materials, foodstuffs, and energy sources in the right areas
is necessary to a rapid expansion of both world output and
world trade.

3. To a large extent this can be brought about by reduction of barriers to trade and an extension of the normal
operation of the price system.

4. The contribution to this end of the Bretton Woods
organizations including the General Agreement on Tariffs
and Trade has been large, and this course of action should

be pushed as far as possible—immediately, of course, through participation in the Organization for Trade Cooperation.

5. But Bretton Woods has been able to do what has been done largely because of a continuous flow of United States dollars under special programs essentially regional in character.

6. The result of both international and regional efforts has been the emergence of a postwar trading system that has certainly facilitated growth in various large areas of the world.

7. This trading system, however, is vulnerable in a number of respects. Its continuous existence, on a current—but not altogether satisfactory—plateau depends on the maintenance of prosperity in the United States, a keeping in line of inflationary tendencies, and a continuous lubrication through special flows of United States dollars. The system could be seriously disrupted by curtailment of Middle Eastern oil supplies and by Soviet trade and investment.

8. Even if none of these malign influences impinge, the system is not adequate to support a satisfactory rate of growth in certain large underdeveloped areas of the world.

This brings us finally to an essential element in world economic growth; the problem of the underdeveloped areas. I shall have to content myself with a few bold assertions and a few pertinent questions. While it is obvious that there are many requirements, other than capital and foreign exchange, for economic growth in say, Southern Asia, I am convinced that this area can effectively use much larger assistance than it is now receiving, and that a politically satisfactory rate of growth is dependent on the receipt of additional assistance. The second Indian Plan projects a foreign exchange deficit of about $1.6 billion over the next five years, and a similar projection for Pakistan would yield a figure of $500 million to $600 million. One does not have to accept all the principles and policy decisions on which these projections are based to conclude that some substantial increase in foreign exchange is essential to effective development. I am also convinced, and have argued elsewhere, that a sizable expansion of technical and economic assistance to under-developed areas is very much in the Western interest.[6] The administration, in proposing a slight increase in develop-ment assistance, has indicated that if armament expenditures can be cut, this assistance should be substantially increased.

Even if we assume, however, that aid to underdeveloped areas is substantially increased, there are certain questions regarding its use that have a direct bearing on our own central problem, the expanding requirements of world eco-nomic growth.

First, must we in competition with Soviet offers of assist-ance without strings, abjure any attempt to influence the direction of investment? If Afghanistan wants a steel mill, do we offer to put up a steel mill in Kabul on the ground that if we do not, the Soviet Union will, regardless whether it makes sense to do so?

Second, with the process of investment so largely in state hands and to some extent thereby escaping the influence of economic calculation, will increased assistance defeat rather than promote any tendency toward a balanced expansion of world output of foodstuffs, raw materials, and manufactures? With most of the underdeveloped areas of the world con-fronted by rapid population growth, a concentration on in-dustrial expansion at the expense of foodstuffs and raw materials could produce disastrous consequences.

Third, will the independently determined development processes of various countries lead to serious duplication and, consequently, excess capacity in certain lines accompanied by deficiencies in others? Will the Indian-Pakistan raw jute and jute fabrics situation be multiplied?

All these questions raise the awkward problem of guid-

[6] E. S. Mason, *Promoting Economic Development* (1955).

ance (if you prefer a good word) or intervention (if you prefer a bad one) with respect to foreign aid programs. It would seem to me that the central principle we have to adhere to is that foreign aid is designed to promote economic growth in the expectation that such growth is conducive to social and political developments favorable to the expansion and cohesion of the non-Communist world. If this is not so, I do not know how the case for foreign economic assistance can be stated. If it is so, it means that we cannot afford to let ourselves compete with the Soviet Union on projects that may disrupt rather than promote economic development. If it is so, we cannot afford to neglect the adverse effects on world trade of an unbalanced process of economic development or one that wastes resources through serious duplication of existing facilities.

These are, of course, wastes that in the main would be avoided by private economic calculation. It is my own view, shared I should suppose by most Americans, that the contribution of private dollars to balanced economic development is a multiple of that of public dollars. I should also hold that, in promoting development, a dollar loan from the International Bank for Reconstruction and Development is worth several dollars of grants from the United States Government. Obviously, therefore, we have a strong interest in helping to open up all possible opportunities for investment to private lenders and the International Bank. Beyond this we have an interest in influencing the course of governmental directed investment into channels consistent with balanced growth. We are much more likely to be able to move in both directions if we can develop a foreign aid program of a size and character that gives promise of making a real contribution to the economic prosperity of underdeveloped areas.

5

Asian Co-operation with the West: Conditions and Expectations

HAROLD H. FISHER[1]

THE TITLE of this lecture invites the inference that both Asia and the West are a good deal more united than is actually the case. As a matter of fact the divisions and diversities within both Asia and the West are the first of several circumstances affecting co-operation between Asia and the West to which I wish to direct your attention.

There are many Asias. These Asias have important things in common, but they have many differences. There are many Wests, and though they too have many things in common, they are deeply divided between a free West and a totalitarian West.

A second circumstance is that the Asian countries have entered into what is called the society of independent and equal states in a time of swift revoluntionary changes unequaled in human history. These revolutionary changes have produced a third circumstance by bringing to an end the system of classical imperialism that has governed Asian-Western relations for three centuries. But along with the break-up of empires and the freeing of colonies has come the rise of a new method by which strong countries gain dominion over the weak through the infiltration and organization of a rigidly disciplined policital association called the Communist Party.

[1] Professor of International Relations, San Francisco State College, and Chairman Emeritus, Hoover Institute and Library, Stanford University.

The author wishes to thank the Asia Foundation for putting certain reports and other materials at his disposal during the preparation of this lecture.

A fourth aspect of these revolutionary times concerns economic relations and the seemingly unanimous desire of Asians to share in the advances in productivity and welfare through scientific and technological development. These advances have been made in some countries, for example in the United States and the United Kingdom, by a mixture of private and public enterprise; in other countries they have been accomplished by totalitarian methods and rigid control of consumption, forced capital formation and investment, and a government monopoly of foreign trade.

Finally, this twentieth century revolution has brought the peoples of Asia closer to each other as well as closer to the West. This has deepened old issues and created new ones, including the need for the expansion of cultural exchange. It has sharpened the problems of tolerance and intolerance, of education and propaganda.

For the reasons I shall give you, these circumstances seem to indicate that the nature of Asian co-operation with the West will depend on the degree to which the free West and the totalitarian West observe the principles of peace, equality, and mutuality in their relations with the Asians.

I shall speak about Asian diversity and unity in a moment. I wish first to remind you that although we have become accustomed to speak of relations between the Soviet Union and its satellites and the United States and its allies as "East-West" relations or "East-West" trade, we must not forget that actually in relations between Asia and the West, Soviet Russia belongs with the West. When Mr. Khrushchev declared "We Russians are Asians too!" he was allowing the salesman's warmth of enthusiasm for his line of goods to make him overlook the facts. Russian culture is Occidental not Oriental. The character of the Russian state and its social institutions were formed in five centuries of struggle to resist invasions from Asia across the broad Eurasian steppes. The Orthodox Church, as the guardian of the Russian culture and national spirit, survived and gained strength during the two centuries the Mongols ruled Russia.

Later Russia, like her European neighbors, became an imperialist power, a conqueror and ruler of Asian peoples. Unlike the other European imperialists, the Russians became colonizers of Asian lands, and the people of those lands became Russian subjects. The Imperial Government treated both Russian settlers and native peoples of its Asian provinces as colonies of the metropolis. Russia, like China—which was also a colonizer in Asia—remained economically underdeveloped despite the considerable investment of European capital. For geographical and historical reasons, Imperial Russia became more eastern than its European neighbors. Many Russian leaders believed Russia's destiny lay in uniting with peasant Asia against industrial Europe. Many Asians today think of Soviet imperialism as less harsh and Russian ways less alien than those of Europe and North America. Perhaps this is in part because the Asian subjects of Russia have had less opportunity than the people of European colonies to express their opinion of their Imperial and Soviet masters.

The Communists are the promoters of a Western heresy —Marxism. They have revolted against Western political, economic, and social institutions. That revolt having been partially successful, the Communists proclaimed a kind of armistice, which has gone under various names: "Socialism in one country," "the theory of the two camps," "peaceful coexistence." They have, in a sense, seceded from the West and now seek to draw the countries of Asia into association with the secessionist Communist bloc. In this shift of interest toward Asia, the Soviet Communists are again following in the steps of their Tsarist predecessors in turning toward Asia when they have been checked in the West.

Asian Diversities

In their relations with the West, the Asians are more likely to speak with one voice than to act as one man. The Asians I have in mind live chiefly in the regions east and south of Afghanistan—in the regions familiarly known as East Asia, Southeast Asia and South Asia. I shall refer only incidentally to Western Asia—the Middle East and Russian Central Asia. The diversities of Asia are innumerable, and they criss-cross in every direction. The great world religions—Buddhism, Hinduism, Islam, Confucianism, Zoroastrianism, Christianity —are all represented, over-flowing political and national boundaries.

Language diversity is more complex though not perhaps more deeply divisive than religion. All of the larger countries and some of the smaller ones are multi-lingual. India alone, according to the old British census, has 222 languages. Of these 222, twelve are major languages and the mother tongues of over 95 per cent of the Indian population.

The linguistic diversity of China, which was reputed to be the home of between forty and fifty languages and dialects, used to be expressed in the old joke that a Cantonese and a Shanghaiese must converse in English if at all. It is worth observing that the official languages of the Asian-African conference at Bandung in 1955 were English and French.

In Indonesia the linguistic diversity is equally great and the geography of the archipelago is an invitation to diversity. The people are of Malay stock. They speak about 250 different languages.

In Burma and the Indo-Chinese states, the situation is almost as complex; in the Philippines and Thailand and Ceylon, nearly so. Not the least of these national or tribal problems results from the division of these linguistic groups among two or several different states. For example, there are Mongols in China and the Soviet Union as well as in Outer Mongolia; the Thais of Thailand have relatives in China, Cambodia, Laos, and Viet Nam; the Malays are found in Indonesia, Thailand, and the Philippines as well as in Malaya. As one of the leading American authorities on the area has observed, it is evident that "the range and variety of peoples and cultures are truly unmatched anywhere else on earth." The Chinese and Indians have created no less serious problems by their migrations. The Chinese in Indonesia, Malaya, Thailand, Viet Nam, Burma, and the Philippines and the Indians in Burma, Malaya, and Ceylon have had and will continue to have great influence on the relations of these smaller states with their larger neighbors, China and India.

The Asians are divided not only vertically by language, religion, nationality, and other cultural traits but also horizontally by classes and castes. The Asia we are considering contains social institutions representative of almost every stage of development known to historians and anthropologists. In every Asian country, a small educated urban minority directs the affairs of a vast illiterate rural majority. A part of but separate from this illiterate majority, there are in some countries the untouchables, who in spite of their legal liberation are still in considerable numbers the objects of segregation and other discriminations in India, Korea, Japan, and Tibet.

The fact that untouchability still exists in different forms in some Asian countries is not only evidence of diversity but proof that it takes time and something more than laws to eliminate long-established practices of discrimination and segregation in Asia as well as in America. In a great part of rural Asia the villagers live isolated lives unaware of and uninterested in what goes on in another village five miles distant and equally unaware, we may be sure, of the issues involved in co-operation with the West. Like the villages, Asian countries have also been isolated from each other. When an Indian delegation visited China in 1951, the Chinese protocol speeches referred to this as repaying the visits of the Chinese Buddhist pilgrims to India in the fifth and seventh centuries.

Asian Similarities

With all these diversities, the Asians have enough important things in common not only to justify our consideration of the question of Asian co-operation but also to make it our duty to do so. Objective conditions show many similarities. Over 70 per cent of Asians live in villages. Most of them have some form of the extended family system and many similar traditions and institutions relating to property, economic co-operation, and local government. With the notable exception of Japan, they are raw-material countries whose prosperity has come in a large measure to depend on the state of the world market in respect to rice, tin, petroleum, jute, rubber, copra, and so forth; and all—again with the exception of Japan—are economically underdeveloped and have—except for Japan and Ceylon—low literacy. All have low life expectancy and great poverty. All belong to the non-Caucasian races.

From the point of view of this discussion, the most important elements of unity are subjective. The Asians do not have that "common national memory" that Denis Brogan has spoken of,[2] but all have national memories of similar experience in past relations with the West. And they have a "common set of problems and inherited difficulties." All have been subject to a greater or less degree to Western dominion and to racial or other kinds of discrimination. All except Japan have been colonies or semi-colonies of the West.

The urban elites who today rule Asian countries have

[2] See above, p. 39.

similar goals, similar hopes, and fears for the future. These leaders have been exposed to such Western revolutionary ideas as nationalism, political democracy, social welfare, the labor movement, Marxism, and most lately Russian communism.

Most Asian leaders are concerned lest their new-found independence be lost in some new and subtle colonialism. As a great many Asian intellectuals accept such Marxist-Leninist theories of international relations as the class nature of the state, the law of uneven development, and imperialism as the highest stage of capitalism, they are more suspicious of the intentions of foreign capitalists than of foreign Communists. The great dilemma of the Asian leaders is that while they are uncertain of the intentions of the foreigners, they are dependent on foreign capital, capital goods, and technology for that modernization of their ways that all believe will raise Asian levels of living and bring a larger share of the benefits of scientific advances. Asians often say that they have much to learn, especially from the Russians who have so recently experienced the transformation the Asians wish to accomplish.

Asia and the Twentieth Century Revolution

The Asians gained their independence and took their first steps as sovereign and equal members of the society of nations straight into the midst of a world revolution of vast scope and incalcuable consequences. Every aspect of international relations has a new dimension. This enlargement of all problems in human relations has taken place just when the newly liberated Asian countries have assumed the task of transforming the political, economic, and social institutions inherited from colonial days. As the former colonies take up this formidable job, they find that the countries with more experience in self-government are themselves uncertain, as they are forced to create new institutions and improvise new procedures to deal with problems of the twentieth century revolution. There is no single well-explored path, straight and clear, for the Asians to follow. While the Asians are trying to catch up with the West, they must also try to solve the new problems that the atomic age is forcing the West to face.

I shall not attempt to discuss either the scientific or the economic effects of this atomic revolution on Asian-Western relations. I should, however, like to invite your attention to three consequences of this revolutionary situation that seem to me to bear on the conditions and expectations of Asian co-operation with the West.

One of these circumstances is the ambivalence of the Asian intellectuals, who as the new ruling class are formulating the aims and terms of this co-operation. The Indonesian novelist, Takdir Alisjahbana, says that this ambivalence is due to the fact that because of their education they are in the modern age and because of their birth they live in a country that is still dominated by a traditional national culture. "Asia," he says, "is living in thirty centuries at one and the same time. The Stone Age lives alongside the Machine Age, mediaeval feudalism and mysticism battle modern democracy and rationalism, and communalism and economic planning jostle each other daily."[3] The Asian must participate in the modern world, which requires a broad international outlook, and at the same time he is a part of his own nation, a majority of whose members are clinging to old traditions. The Asian intellectual, says Mr. Alisjahbana, vacillates between two crises: that of the Asian community and culture in contact with the West, and the world crisis affecting all mankind, whose values are threatened by a "tide of secularism, scepticism and relativism."

Prime Minister Nehru has also written about this prob-

[3] "Traditional and Modern Values in Our Culture," in Herbert Passin, ed. *Cultural Freedom in Asia* (1956), p. 40.

lem of the Asian intellectuals, who, he says, learned to think "like British intellectuals" and so gained some understanding of the modern world. This was well enough, but the intellectuals were cut off from the masses who continued to think as Asians. But now, says Pandit Nehru, "this faith in Western thought is itself being shaken, and so we have neither the old nor the new, and we drift not knowing whither we are going." He observes that these may be the inevitable consequences of an age of transition, but he adds that they may be serious because "in the atomic age no country is likely to be given many chances to correct itself, and failure may well mean disaster."[4]

Another consequence of the twentieth century revolution is that it is becoming harder and harder to separate the internal issues of a single country from its international issues; that is to say, that more and more the chief internal issues of one country are linked with the internal issues of other countries. This is particularly true of economic matters. Recently communities in the cotton producing sections of the United States have adopted resolutions urging a boycott against Japanese textiles, and the legislatures of those states in the Deep South have passed laws discriminating against Japanese goods imported into this country. To the citizens of these southern communities anything that effects the price of cotton would appear to be a local issue. It is, but it is also an international issue. The United States, it is true, has a surplus of cotton. But it is also true that Japan is one of the largest buyers of American raw cotton.

Moreover, since Japan must sell its products abroad in order to buy raw materials and food on which to live, the actions of these southern communities are calculated to influence Japan to turn away from the United States and look elsewhere for the exchange of goods on which it must depend. The Soviet Union obviously would be delighted to

[4] Introduction to R. D. Sinha Dinkar, *Four Phases of Culture* (1956), quoted in *The New Republic* (Mar. 19, 1956), p. 7.

have Japan make such a decision. And the Soviet bloc would undoubtedly offer to provide markets and the raw materials the Japanese need. In fact, the Communists would consider this snarl in the trade relations between Japan and the United States as further support of the Communist belief in the incapacity of the competitive private enterprise system to deal with the international economic problems of the twentieth century.

The Communists ever since Karl Marx have been notorious for their underestimation of the resourcefulness of freedom of enterprise and freedom of thought. The ability of the free world to avoid the postwar economic collapse predicted by the Communists and to restore productivity and even unprecedented prosperity has not passed unnoticed in the Asian countries that have also benefited by the creative achievements of free enterprise. But the Asian countries realize that in the West these achievements have been emergency measures, and the problems of international economic co-operation and interchange remain unsolved. In the meantime the United States produces food surpluses, while many people in friendly countries go hungry. This situation, I take it, is a consequence of the twentieth century revolution. The Communists claim to have a solution; the free West is still looking for one.

The Asians will remain in some doubt about the possibilities of co-operation with the free West until we have devised new procedures and institutions that will facilitate the exchange of goods, services, and ideas, which these revolutionary changes seem to call for. Asians would, I believe, be encouraged if as much progress were being made in the old problems of economic co-operation and interchange as has been made in the new problem of the uses of atomic energy through President Eisenhower's atoms for peace proposals, the projected international atomic agency, and the atomic research centers in Asia.

In the meantime, the claims of the Soviet Communists that

they have the answers to all problems of the atomic age are calculated to appeal in two ways to the Asians. First, the Communists have their own concrete proposals for economic co-operation and interchange. I shall refer to this again later. Second, the Communists have worked out a powerfully attractive formula for these young Asians who, according to Nehru, have "no standards left, nothing to direct their thinking or control their action."

On the operational side, moreover, the Communists have developed methods of organization and propaganda that are effective means of protest against political frustrations and economic conditions; and in Asia there are many things to protest about. They have perfected ways of organizing and disciplining the discontented and of using the democratic freedoms of association, speech, and opinion to seize power in economically underdeveloped and politically inexperienced countries.

Communists and other totalitarians have shown that by using their power to force their people to consume less, work harder, and invest more, they can increase industrial output faster than Western states, which have concentrated on increasing the standard of living and preserving freedom. *Lloyds Bank Review* has calculated that in 1950, the industrial output of the Soviet Union was about 35 per cent of that of the United States, but that in 1955 it had risen to nearly 50 per cent. Those who made this calculation accept the possibility that Soviet industrial output might equal that of the United States by 1963.[5]

This development significantly affects Asian relations with the West because Asians believe that they must industrialize in the shortest possible time. Soviet economic growth does not prove the truth of the Communist dogma that capitalism contains the seeds of its own destruction, but it tends to dis-

[5] Quoted by Harold Callender in "Soviet's Rising Economy," *New York Times,* Apr. 15, 1956.

prove the capitalist assumption that the private enterprise system is vastly more productive than the collectivist. If capital and technical aid are unavailable in the free West, some of the Asian countries will be greatly tempted to look to the Soviet Union and China and follow the Communist path of using taxes or forced loans or price control to divert the product of the people's labor from consumption to investment in production.

Another significant Communist transformation has to do with the ideas of peace and nationalism. Peace is one of the great objectives of the Asian elites. Nationalism is one of the strongest political forces in Asia. Asian pacifism is deeply embedded in the religious beliefs of Hinduism and Buddhism. Asian nationalism is an importation from the West that quickly took root and was strengthened by the growing opposition to Western imperialism. It was also stimulated by the policies of the first Asian country to adopt Western ways. Over a half century ago at the time of the European "scramble for concessions" and spheres of influence in China, Japan became a champion of the slogan "Asia for the Asians." Japan gave encouragement to Asian nationalism by its defeat of Russia in the war of 1904-05. In the First World War—called by the Indian historian and diplomatist, Sardar Panikkar, "the European civil war"— Asian nationalism was greatly encouraged by the fact that the imperialist powers were forced to call on their colonies for aid. They were heartened by Woodrow Wilson's eloquent championship of self-determination. Japan gave further aid to Asian nationalism in the Second World War by overthrowing the British, French, Dutch, and American power in East and Southeast Asia, by recognizing and arming the Asian nationalists, and then, in reverse, by provoking local nationalisms in resistance to Japanese oppression.

The Communists are not pacifists and they are not nationalists, but they have championed peace and nationalism as means to their ends. For many years before and after their seizure of power, they denounced religious and philosophic pacifism as muddle-headed sentimentalism. They denounced nationalism with equal vehemence as a trick of the ruling classes to control the toiling and exploited masses and as a deception to prepare them for war.

To the Communist some wars were not only justifiable, but necessary as a means of overthrowing the ruling class and of liberating the masses and defending them from and against their class enemies. While organizing "partisans of peace" and circulating the Stockholm peace petition, the Communists have organized and led armed forces in civil and guerrilla wars throughout East, South, and Southeast Asia. The Communists have championed peace, not because war was evil or unnecessary, but only because it brought death and suffering to the wrong people.

The Communists have also been champions of self-determination and the liberation of all colonies, but with three important reservations. The right of revolution took precedence over the right of self-determination; second, the right of self-determination could legitimately be exercised only by the party of the proletariat, that is, the Communist party; and, third, the Asian colonies of the Soviet Union were not included among the peoples to be freed from Western imperialist rule.

The revolution in Communist tactics proclaimed by the Twentieth Congress of the Communist Party of the Soviet Union officially repudiated the dogma of inevitable war. The spectacular pilgrimage of Khrushchev and Bulganin to India, Burma, and Afghanistan in 1955 seems to have been designed to dramatize the change in tactics from a world-wide class struggle to a world-wide movement for peace and economic development. Another purpose was to shift the focus of Asian nationalism from political independence to economic independence from the free West. A third purpose

was to reassert Soviet leadership of the Communist movement, which had been threatened by the failure of Stalin's
policies in Asia, by the consolidation and growing prestige
of the Chinese People's Government and the increase in its
influence in Asia. After the death of Stalin, no Communist
could rival the position of Mao Tse-tung as the world's most
eminent revolutionary leader.

The new tactics of "trade not aid," "aid without strings,"
and "peaceful coexistence" are undoubtedly more popular
in Asia than the dogmas of the class war, but they do not
erase the significance of the fact that there are now two
centers of power in the Communist movement. One of these
centers is Western and is in Moscow, and one is Asian and
is in Peking. The Communist system has no place for two
posts of command. Collective leadership is not a group of
equals. One, more equal than the rest, must be at the top
of the chain of command. The solution of these problems
will take time, create tensions within the Communist camp,
and greatly affect the course of events in Asia. In the meantime, perhaps, we should remember that although Stalinism
has been denounced and repudiated, the doctrines and the
organization from which Stalinism grew remain. We should
also take account of the probability that if Soviet tactics were
to be revolutionized, as they are now alleged to have been,
such a change would be accomplished by some such revolution from above as has taken place.

Attitudes of Asian Leaders

The Asian nations have not adopted a common foreign
policy nor formed a regional organization in spite of some
tentative moves in that direction. But their foreign policies,
official declarations, and the resolutions of regional con-
ferences, particularly the Bandung Conference in April 1955,
reveal certain attitudes that Asian leaders, with some excep-

tions, share. These attitudes show that the Asians want and expect to co-operate with the West, if possible with both the free West and the totalitarian West. The free West appears to possess more of what the Asians want and need, but at this moment the totalitarian West appears to be making its less substantial offers with fewer strings and on more generous terms.

It will be convenient to consider these attitudes toward co-operation under the three principles that I have already mentioned: peace, equality, and mutuality. Asians unquestionably prefer to seek for peace and security through the observance of the principles of the United Nations and through the use of United Nations agencies and by negotiation, conciliation, arbitration, or judicial settlement in accordance with the Charter. It is certain that Asians would not co-operate in isolationist or nationalistic policies aimed at limiting or weakening the influence of the United Nations. They favor membership for all qualified countries, and they would like a larger representation on the Security Council for the Asia-Africa region.

The Asians have recognized the right of collective self-defense but with restrictions. Regional security measures should not be used, they say, to serve the interests of the great powers or to exert pressure on smaller powers. A great many Asian leaders believe world tensions are caused by the struggle for power between the Soviet Union and the United States. They have little faith in military alliances, power blocs, or armament programs. A great many believe that the duty of Asia is to follow an independent policy, a third way between the two power blocs, to work for universal disarmament and for the prohibition of production or use of or experimentation with nuclear and thermonuclear weapons. In some Asian countries, such as Japan and the Philippines, the danger of Communist military aggression is taken more seriously than in other parts of Asia, but even there the problem of national security is considered less urgent than problems of, as they say, social security and international economic co-operation and exchange.

Most Asian countries deplore the refusal of the United States to have political and economic relations with the Communist People's Government of China. That policy has not weakened the Communists nor contributed to the security of China's Asian neighbors, many of whom have recognized the Peking government and carry on economic and cultural relations with it. Moreover, Asian intellectuals have great respect for China's past and cultural achievements. Under the Communists, and by methods that we thoroughly disapprove, China has recovered the position of a great power with disconcerting speed. The thousands of Asians who have been streaming into China as visitors these last two or three years or who have been reading the Communist accounts of China's revival have been impressed not so much by the achievements of communism as by the achievements of a great Asian country that has many of the same problems as other Asian countries. The costs to the Chinese people of these accomplishments are drowned out in the noisy acclamation of China's industrialization.

The professions of peaceful intentions and the continuous advocacy of peaceful coexistence by Peking and Moscow appear to the Asian mind in strong contrast to the stiff refusal of the United States to co-operate in what is alleged to be a sincere effort to relieve tensions and promote peace and welfare in Asia. Unquestionably, influential Asian leaders regard the United States policy of nonrecognition and trade embargo as a phase of the struggle for power. They would welcome the admission of Red China to the United Nations and the extension of Sino-American negotiations on the issues of Korea and Formosa Straits as a step toward peace.

Western opinion has been baffled by what appears to be an Asian inclination to be more worried about the free West, which in recent years has been liberating its colonies, than about the totalitarian West in which Communist "liberation" has meant subordination of large areas to the Soviet Union or to the Chinese People's Government. Some Asians, however, have also been concerned about the intentions of Communist China and its Soviet ally. There is reason to believe that South Asians would feel more secure if the People's Government were to tighten its ties with its Asian neighbors and loosen them with the Soviet Union. Professor George Kahin argues convincingly that the five Asian sponsors of the Bandung Conference hoped that such a meeting would provide an occasion to work for three things: the avoidance of war between Red China and the United States over the Formosa Straits issues, the encouragement of China's diplomatic independence of the U.S.S.R. and the containment of Chinese Communist influence in the Indo-Chinese states and in other south Asian countries.

No estimate of the situation is complete that fails to take into account the complexities of the relations of Communist China with its neighbors, especially those with Chinese minorities, or overlooks the significance to China of the ambition of the Soviet Union to be Big Brother to all Asia.

The Asian desire for equality, the second of the three principles I have mentioned, is expressed in several ways, the most significant being those rights associated with nationalism and self-determination. The first four of the ten principles adopted by the representatives of the twenty-nine nations in the final communiqué at Bandung ask for respect for fundamental human rights, for the sovereignty and integrity of all nations, recognition of the equality of all races and of all nations large and small, and abstention from intervention or interference in the internal affairs of another country.

This emphasis on equality is part of the Asian resentment against colonialism past, present, and potential. Incidentally, it also runs counter to the hierarchical principle applied by the Communists in their international relations within the Communist bloc and within the Soviet Union. There is only one "first land of socialism" and that is the U.S.S.R. People's democracies are followers not equals. At the head of the Communist nationalities comes "the great Russian people." The Chinese are also accorded the title "great," but the others are assigned positions of rank according to some Soviet system of computation and with the same careful precision that members of the Presidium of the Russian Communist Party are arranged in order of precedence along the top of Lenin's tomb on the first of May.

Neutralism is related to the strong desire for peace and to religious pacifism. It is also related to the principle of equality, the spirit of pride and self-respect that is on guard against foreign dictation, that is resentful whenever Asians are not consulted when the great powers are deciding Asian issues. If there is anything Asia wants to tell the world, said Nehru in his closing speech at Bandung, it is that there is going to be no dictation in the future, no yes-men in Asia. He went on to say that Asians want to be friends and to co-operate with Europe and America, but, he continued, "we shall only co-operate in the future as equals; there is no friendship when nations are not equal, when one has to obey the other and when one dominates the other. That is why we raise our voice against domination and colonialism from which many of us have suffered so long and that is why we have to be careful to see that any other form of domination does not come our way."[6] Nehru has had enough experience with communism in India to give point to his warning against "any other form of domination."

President Sukarno in his opening address not only made his much quoted reference to Paul Revere's ride as the begin-

[6] George McT. Kahin, *The Asian-African Conference: Bandung, Indonesia, April 1955* (1956), p. 44.

ning of the "first successful anti-colonial war in history" but he also warned that "colonialism has also its modern dress, in the form of economic control, intellectual control, actual physical control by a small but alien community within a nation."[7]

Other delegates at Bandung warned more forcefully and directly that Asians and Africans should be as much opposed to Soviet colonialism as to Western imperialism. It is unlikely, however, that the issue of Communist colonialism will be clearly drawn unless and until the United States and its allies take a clear and unequivocal position that the age of colonialism is past, that within a specified time all colonies shall be freed, and that every land capable of self-government shall have it.

Asian Modernization

Asians are as united in their desire for the modernization of their economic institutions as in their opposition to colonialism. The expectations based on this desire create a complex system of interlocking dilemmas. They need help in the form of capital and technical aid, but they do not intend to become the objects of charity. Nor do they like to pay for foreign aid by subordinating their policies to those of their benefactors. Asians also realize that no amount of capital and technical aid will bring about economic development unless they have a supporting system of values. This creates another dilemma, for this means that the Asian systems of values must be changed, and Asian leaders are greatly worried lest the changes caused by industrialism result in the destruction of Eastern values they cherish and in the introduction of Western values they reject.

These dilemmas relate to both economic and cultural relations and there is no perfect solution. The best course for

[7] *Ibid.*

the free West would seem to be to recognize and demonstrate that the purpose of these relations is not to serve the exclusive interests of the donor and the recipient but to advance the cause of world peace, progress and freedom. The most successful methods will be those based on the principle of mutuality, on the realization that the Asians as well as the West have much to contribute to the common long-range objectives and that ways must be devised whereby these contributions from both sides can be made jointly and effectively.

The Asians need foreign aid and markets for their raw materials. They hope for this aid without attached strings that would tie them to the foreign policy of a particular country, or to the private enterprise system, or to totalitarianism.

The recent Soviet offers of aid have three interesting features. They offer to provide the services of technicians along with the equipment supplied to the contracting government. The Soviet Union also will give training in the U.S.S.R. to foreign technicians from the contracting countries and usually in connection with the purchase of Soviet equipment. The Soviet Government does not make a grant but requires payment on reasonable terms for the technical aid as well as the equipment. This system is very much like that by which many well-known American industrial and engineering concerns sold the equipment and technical knowledge to the Soviet Union at the beginning of its program of rapid industrialization during the first Five Year Plan. The goods and skills the Russians are now offering for export are, in a sense, the product of the skills and equipment imported by the Soviet Union from the United States and Western Europe twenty-five or thirty years ago.

The second feature of the Soviet aid program is that the Asians are given the opportunity of paying for what they receive by the sale to the Communist bloc of the raw materials and agricultural products of which the contracting country may have a surplus. The Soviet Government can do this without any fear that a deputy to the Supreme Soviet from a Central Asian Soviet Republic will object on the ground that aid to Egypt or Pakistan may enable those countries to compete with the Soviet cotton growers.

Third, the Soviet Government does not make these aid and trading operations contingent on the signing of a military preparedness agreement or joining a regional or other security pact. The Communists at this stage are not trying to make these Asians into Communists but to detach them from the free West and draw them into what they innocuously call an area of peace and development.

These policies emphasize the dangers in United States policy that attaches military and political strings to foreign aid and that subordinates economic and foreign policy to the immediate interests of producers in individual states 'or regions of the United States.

If we wish to preserve freedom in the world we must preserve the membership of the free world. To do that, we must find ways to take into account not only the well-being of owners, managers, and employees of American enterprises but also the well-being of the owners (whether public or private), managers, and employees of Japan and Burma and Malaya and other countries of the free world. This observation, if it ever gets that far, will not be well received on Capitol Hill. The Congress has trouble enough with the competing economic interests of different regions of the United States without extending the area of conflict to include foreigners. The Communists contend that capitalism is incapable of adjusting such conflicts, and the new Soviet foreign economic policy is aimed at driving home the soundness of this Communist contention.

The urgency of the challenge depends on the ability of the Communist bloc to supply the equipment, including arms and technical skills, the Asians need. For nearly forty years we have been underestimating the ability of a totalitarian collectivist system to produce goods and scientists and engineers. We now may be in danger of overestimating both the quantity and the quality of the Communist output. I am easily intimidated by statistics, and I am impressed by the reports of the rate of increase of Soviet production. I am not much reassured by another estimate that the total capital made available to the entire world by the Soviet Union in 1955 was only about one tenth of the amount now requested by the President from the Congress for non-military aid to Asia.

Several proposals have been made on the best way to meet this Communist challenge. One is for the United States to give less of its support in bilateral arrangements and more by support of United Nations programs such as the Special United Nations Fund for Economic Development, the programs of the specialized agencies and through such regional arrangements as the Colombo Plan. Congressman Brooks Hays, a Democrat, and Congressman Chester C. Merrow, a Republican, both United States delegates to the Tenth Session of the United Nations General Assembly, have given bipartisan support to the United Nations multilateral assistance program on the sound basis that the purpose of foreign aid is not to purchase affection, which cannot be bought at any price, but "to strengthen the free world, eliminating the vacuums of weakness into which the Soviet power is trying to move."[8]

The Director General of the Japanese Economic Planning Board has suggested the formation of an Asian Development Corporation financed equally by the United States and the participating Asian countries. Governor Averell Harriman has proposed the formation of an international lending authority with more flexibility than the International Bank. The Soviet Union would be invited to join as a test of both its sincerity and its capacity to take part in such an

[8] *New York Times,* Mar. 29, 1956.

undertaking for other than propaganda purposes. The Committee for Economic Development approves the establishment of an International Finance Corporation as an affiliate of the International Bank, to invest in private undertakings with private investors in underdeveloped countries. The committee also believes in an expanded program of public investment in underdeveloped countries.

The Asians have resented the idea some Americans have done their best to promulgate, that the United States has given aid only because of a consuming fear of communism and not for humanitarian reasons or to relieve international tensions and maintain international relations on a basis of equality and mutuality. The new course in Communist tactics may be more effective than the protests of the Asians in convincing the free West that the revolution that is transforming most other aspects of life is also transforming international and intercultural relations. Asians are asking the peoples of the free West to be as creative in these matters as they have been in science and technology and administration. We have shown signs of this creative power in such concepts as the Marshall Plan, the Colombo Plan, and Point Four, and in such undertakings as the Joint Committee on Rural Reconstruction in China and community development and joint educational projects in other countries. To have maximum effect and to meet the test of mutuality, the American partners in the free West must carry out these undertakings as joint efforts in which the American capacity to produce surpluses will be applied to raising the levels of living of the underdeveloped areas, not as an emergency measure to defeat Communism, but as a long-term policy suited to this revolutionary age of swift communication and atomic power.

A quarter of a century ago, Rabindranath Tagore called for someone to show the East to the West and convince the West that the East has contributions to make to civilization. This is still true; but the problem has become more complicated as well as more urgent. This is the job of education but of education in its broadest conception.

A recent analysis of Asian studies in United States teacher and undergraduate institutions by the Conference on Asian Affairs Incorporated indicates that 40 per cent of them offer no appreciable opportunities for Asian studies. A survey by the United Nations Educational, Scientific, and Cultural Organization (UNESCO) finds that European students have even fewer opportunities to learn about Asia's history and culture. More courses on Asia can and no doubt will be offered in the universities and colleges of the free West. But this will not be enough.

Ever since men have had cultural values to exchange, they have carried on intercultural relations. In the pursuit of knowledge or profit or power, men have taken long journeys, endured danger and hardship to learn from or impart to others knowledge and skills and methods by which life is enriched or made easier and knowledge increased and diffused. Until very recently, that is until three or four centuries ago, the East has been giving more than it has received. This has now changed. The East is learning the science, the technical, and administrative skills of the West. The United States and the Soviet Union have been the most active in the export of their separate and competing brands of Western ideology and culture. Neither seems to have realized that to be most beneficial to all concerned, intercultural relations should be based on a kind of barter that recognizes that all parties have something of value to exchange.

Many of the innumerable and complex programs carried on by the United States have been of great value to many Asians. But they have sometimes failed because they have been conceived as a selling campaign to sell the American way of life to the Asians and dissuade them from following the false and devious ways of the Communists. These programs have also failed because they did not recognize the values of Asian cultures or realize how imporant knowledge of those cultures is for the conduct of Asian-American relations.

Lack of mutual understanding, as Dr. Grayson Kirk has suggested, is a major obstacle to co-operation between Asia and the free West.[9] The attitudes that stand in the way of this understanding are the result of a long evolutionary process. They are deep seated. But specialists in such matters believe that even deep seated attitudes can be changed by education and cultural contacts. Such contacts are now possible on an unprecedented scale. The totalitarian West is making the most of this fact. The United Nations, UNESCO, and other specialized agencies, as well as the United States Government and several private American institutions, have been carrying on such enterprises.

The university-to-university contracts between fifty-three American universities and colleges and foreign institutions are being carried out under the auspices of the International Cooperation Administration as a supplement to the technical aid program. They should be carried out for their own sake and on a larger scale, as joint research and educational undertakings to help Westerners understand Asia and help Asians understand the West and each other.

The essential condition of this and all other forms of co-operation between Asia and the West is that there shall not be benefactors on one side and beneficiaries on the other but partners in the benefits and burdens of a new age.

[9] See above, p. 17.

6

American Interest in Asian Development

WILLARD L. THORP[1]

IT IS OBVIOUS that one of the great revolutions in man's history is taking place in Asia.[2] Civilizations that had crystallized into fairly static form centuries ago have suddenly become exposed to different ways of life and unfamiliar systems of social values. The comfortable shelter of isolation has been torn away, and rising expectations have taken the place of an unchallenging acceptance of an unchanging *status quo*. The new is struggling with the old as these countries seek to break out of the vicious circles generated by poverty, disease, and ignorance. Political revolutions have already occurred and recurred, the old social patterns are disintegrating, and economic stagnation is under pressure from programs of economic development.

To use "Asia" as a collective noun covers a multitude of differences. Japan began its drive toward modernization some eighty years ago, while many of the other areas in Asia are still carrying on as their ancestors did a thousand years ago. Some countries have developed widespread commercial exchange, while others contain many autarkic subsistence communities. The Asian nations have differing religions, social patterns, forms of government, resource availabilities, and

[1] Director, Merrill Center for Economics, Amherst College.

[2] The word "Asia" will be used in this lecture, in complete disregard of all geographers and atlases, to include the Asian continent from Afghanistan and Pakistan eastward thus excluding the area sometimes called Western Asia and sometimes the Middle East, to include the islands of Ceylon, Indonesia, Japan, and the Philippines, and to be limited to "free" Asia, that is, the countries in this area free of Communist domination.

The word "America" and its derivatives will be used in this lecture to refer to the United States of America.

population pressures. Nevertheless, from the American view, these differences are probably less important than the similarities. All these countries have a wretchedly low level of living. Using that highly inadequate measure, average income per capita, Japan is highest with about $100 per year and the rest range not far from $50 per capita per year (1949). They have social patterns and attitudes that have the strength of centuries of application and conviction. They have new and usually not very efficient forms of government. They have strong feelings of nationalism and independence. And all of them are in the process of sweeping and organic change. It is by no means clear where they will go or how rapidly, but it is certain that they will travel far away from their old social, economic, and political patterns.

Americans cannot help but have a profound interest in this process. The conditions against which these countries are rebelling are conditions that we too regard as enemies— poverty, disease, ignorance, disorder, and dependence. The immediate American response is not the result of some calculated narrow national interest. Rather it is a fundamental human reaction of sympathy and concern. We are deeply interested in Asian development for its own sake.

Nor is it in our nature merely to sit by and watch the play go on. Being concerned, we must take some action. When the Point Four Program was announced, it was greeted with enthusiasm not only by underdeveloped countries. In the United States, it was welcomed by the average citizen not because he would derive any benefit from it, but because it satisfied his fundamental desire to help the peoples in the underdeveloped countries in their efforts to move forward. According to the pollsters, Point Four always had a higher popularity rating than did the Marshall Plan. Thus, underlying all other elements in the consideration of American interest in Asia is a persistent human urge to help in the age-old battle against poverty, disease, and ignorance.

Economic Interests

The American interest in Asian development is by no means limited, however, to this basic sympathy with efforts at improvement *per se*. Certainly, this dimension establishes a propensity to act, but there are many other elements in our relationship that may be supporting or offsetting and need to be considered.

There are at least three angles from which our economic interest should be examined—Asia as a source of raw materials, Asia as a market for American goods, and Asia as an opportunity for American investment. How important are these three elements to the United States today and what is their potential in the future? How much weight should be given them in that totality of considerations that create individual interest and underlie national foreign policy?

Source of Raw Materials

It was Malthus who gave economics the name of the dismal science, by forecasting that misery was assured by the frugality of nature and the multiplicity of man. More recently, the President's Materials Policy Commission has pictured in great detail the prospect that the United States is outgrowing its resource base. It seems quite obvious that further economic expansion here and elsewhere will require an ever-increasing supply of raw materials. To be sure, the record shows that gross national product usually grows more rapidly than the raw material component because of more and more complex fabricating and because of the greater increase in the service categories such as trade and government. Nevertheless, it is clear that our raw material requirements will increase substantially over time.

How important is Asia as a source of raw materials for use in America? When the record is examined, it is surprising to find that the United States demand for imported raw materials has shifted its geographical pattern greatly since prewar days. There has been a marked increase in the import demand for metals, newsprint, petroleum, coffee, and other items obtained primarily from sources in the Western Hemisphere. At the same time, there has been a diminished emphasis on silk and other fibers, tin, and rubber, which comprised the bulk of our prewar import demand from Asian sources. Today, petroleum, newsprint, and copper lead the list of our imports of crude and semimanufactured nonfood materials. Only two from Asia are anywhere near the top of the list—rubber, which is fourth, and tin, which is ninth.

But the category of raw materials includes much more than these few major commodities. In 1953 there were fifty-seven crude and semimanufactured nonfood materials, the import of which from all sources not only exceeded $5 millions in value but also was greater than the United States production. For seventeen of these fifty-seven varieties, an Asian country was the leading supplier. (The detailed data are presented in the table on page 121.) Natural rubber and tin are, of course, on the list. They account for nearly half the imports to the United States from Asia and clearly nothing else is in the same category of importance. Among the other fifteen items, fibres, feathers, and skins account for nine; copra, coconut oil, and lac and shellac for three more; and manganese, mica, and tungsten complete the list. To be sure, such a list does not indicate the full importance to us of Asian sources. Nux vomica comes entirely from Asia but is excluded from the list because its total value is only about $30,000 per year. Castor oil is a much more important import but is not among the seventeen because Brazil outranks India as a source. In a listing of 140 imported materials not limited either by value or importance of imports, so that the bulk of them are small

UNITED STATES IMPORTS OF CRUDE AND SEMIMANU-
FACTURED MATERIALS BY COMMODITIES WITH AN
ASIAN COUNTRY THE PRIMARY SOURCE, 1953[a]

Commodity	Imports		Leading Country of Origin	
	Total (In thousands of dollars)	Percentage of New Supply	Country	Percentage of Imports
Rubber, natural......	331,497	100.0	Indonesia	41.1
Tin.................	258,663	99.9	British Malaya	38.2
Jute burlaps..........	75,543	100.0	India	75.3
Copra..............	57,488	100.0	Philippines	100.0
Raw silk.............	25,960	100.0	Japan	90.1
Abaca or manila......	23,339	100.0	Philippines	67.3
Persian lamb and caracul...............	20,481	100.0	Afghanistan	55.2
Coconut oil..........	18,960	100.0	Philippines	87.7
Jute, unmanufactured.	14,645	100.0	Pakistan	96.9
Hair, cashmere, alpaca, etc................	14,071	100.0	Outer Mongolia	39.1
Lac and shellac.......	9,987	100.0	India	75.4
Goat and kid skins, except furs...........	24,125	95–100	India	27.2
Manganese ore.......	103,549	95.2	India	37.2
Mica, sheet or block...	13,390	94.1	India	70.6
Tungsten............	91,602	75.7	Korea	26.4
Feathers, waterfowl, crude, for beds.....	6,224	72.3	Taiwan	20.5
Reptile skins.........	5,004	over 50	India	27.0

[a] Source: U. S. Department of Commerce, *Contribution of Imports to U. S., Raw Material Supplies*. World Trade Information Service, Pt. 3, No. 55-40 (November 1955).

specialty items such as pawpaw juice or mangrove bark, an Asian country was the primary source for only thirty-one items.

It is difficult to assess the importance of Asian raw materials to the American economy, particularly in terms of the future. Today, discoveries in the laboratory change the pattern of both demand and supply as much or more than new discoveries under ground. The future of natural rubber and the natural fibres, particularly silk, has been greatly altered by the development of synthetics, and the pressure of war shortages and the development of frozen foods have led to new economies in the use of tin. On the other hand, expanded requirements for ferro-alloys have increased the demand for manganese, tungsten, and titanium.

Possible developments within Asia itself must also be considered. The process of industrialization and the lifting of the level of living above subsistence will increase Asia's need for raw materials. And we cannot disregard the universal ambition of underdeveloped countries to industrialize and thus escape what they feel to be the vulnerable and somewhat subservient position of the raw material supplier. There will be more emphasis in their dreams and in their planning on building steel plants than on producing more iron ore for export.

In further considering the importance of Asia to the United States as a source of raw materials, it is important to keep in mind that very few of our imports from Asia are obtainable only in that area, although other areas may not be able to provide alternative supplies of equal quality at present prices. If a shortage should develop, the consequent higher prices would encourage the use of substitutes as well as substitute sources of supply. Under conditions of stress, either could be used, but it would not be easy. Undoubtedly, the American economy, like every other economy, will be better off if it can buy its raw materials from the widest possible area. However, the evidence does not seem to justify the proposition that dependence on Asian raw materials should enter as an important element in determining United States policy toward Asia.

Markets for American Goods

The second economic consideration is the present and prospective importance of Asia as a market for American goods. First, let us look at the record. Using the Department of Commerce data for trade with the Far East,[3] it appears that American exports to this area, excluding military goods, have remained surprisingly steady at about $2 billions per year for the last four years. Within this apparently stable total, however, there have been substantial changes. In 1952 nearly half of our exports to the Far East were agricultural commodities. By 1955 they had dropped to about 35 per cent, the reductions falling almost entirely on wheat and cotton. An off-setting rise has taken place in nonagricultural commodities over a wide range of items, with the notable exception of textiles and petroleum products. (Details by commodity groups are given in the table on page 124.)

The picture of the actual flow of goods gives only little indication of the prospects for the future in normal market terms. The first question is: What effect will economic development have on the Asian market for imports? The decline in the importation of agricultural commodities is a reflection of increased supplies produced within the area. Will the same result for other commodities come from industrialization? Although it may be true that domestic production will supplant imports for various specific products such as textiles, for example, it is probable that advances in the level of living will expand the market and total imports will increase. Economic development involves not only increased capacity to produce but also a broadening of the market, including an increased demand for imported goods. It is no matter of chance that the volume of trade is highest among the more advanced countries; that the leading United States customers are countries such as Canada, England, and Germany. Thus we can anticipate that the gradual increase in purchasing power as productivity rises will be reflected in

[3] The Department has also defied the geographers by using the term "Far East" to include Southern, Southeastern, and Eastern Asia, and Australia and Other Oceania.

UNITED STATES EXPORTS OF LEADING COMMODITIES
TO FAR EAST[a]

(In millions of dollars)

Commodity	1952	1953	1954	1955
Agricultural commodities:				
Grains and preparations.......	453	345	182	192
Fats, oils, and oilseeds[b]........	53	88	90	102
Other foodstuffs[b].............	57	73	76	120
Cotton, unmanufactured.......	307	160	269	188
Tobacco and manufactures[b]....	80	79	74	91
Nonagricultural commodities:[c]				
Machinery...................	302	333	348	349
Automobiles, parts, and accessories.....................	90	92	98	106
Chemicals and related products.	117	125	142	171
Textile manufactures[d].........	159	175	136	102
Iron and steel—mill products...	50	46	62	98
Petroleum products..........	101	79	69	66
Coal and related products......	30	35	27	34
Copper and copper base alloys..	7	21	38	14
Other commodities.............	242	259	281	358
Total exports to Far East[e].....	2,048	1,908	1,891	1,992
Total exports to all countries.....	15,201	15,774	15,106	15,518

[a] Source: U. S. Department of Commerce, *Foreign Commerce Weekly*, May 9, 1955 and April 30, 1956. Includes Southern, Southeastern and Eastern Asia and Australia and Other Oceania.
[b] Includes certain items not classified as agricultural.
[e] Excluding "special category" items.
[d] Includes a small item of unmanufactured wool and hair.

Asia in terms of a demand for such domestic products as are available, and also for an increasing supply of imported goods. In the immediate future, available foreign exchange will undoubtedly be used in large part for those capital goods that are needed for the development process.

However, a general expansion in import demand does not necessarily mean more trade with the United States. This country is not the only source to which Asian importers can turn. The present $2 billion figure does not represent in any true manner the real prospects for American trade. It must be remembered that American exports to Asian countries last year were financed in considerable part by nearly $800 million of economic assistance. Without such aid, our exports would have been much lower.

On the other hand, there was undoubtedly an additional unexpressed demand that was suppressed by quantitative restrictions on trade and foreign exchange controls. Thus in 1955, exports to Korea increased as economic grants to that country were increased, while shipments to Japan fell off, reflecting restrictions on dollar imports imposed by the Japanese Government late in 1954. Obviously, the limits on American exports to Asia are set under present conditions not by demands by Asian consumers but by the availability of dollars for payment.

The prospects for Asian countries earning more dollars directly is, of course, closely related to the possibility of increased sales to the United States. This will depend in part on various United States policy decisions. While it is difficult to visualize a greatly increased flow from many Asian countries, the recent record has shown that Japan at least has such capabilities. The issue that this raises will be discussed later in terms of tariff policy. In general, suffice it to say that there is no immediate prospect that tariffs will be altered in such a way as to open up large new markets in the United States. In fact, it will take considerable courage and political skill for the administration to hold them down to their present levels on critical commodities.

There may be a greater possibility that Asian countries will be able to obtain dollars in exchange for other currencies that they find easier to earn. This would require substantial progress being made toward more widespread currency convertibility. In the past, a considerable part of international trade was made possible by triangular or multilateral exchanges of goods and currencies. At the present time, only slow but still perceptible progress is being made in this direction.

After considering all these points, the most likely conclusion seems to be that most of such expansion as there
will be in Asian demand for manufactured goods will be
met not by exports from America, but by increased trade
within the area with Japan acting as a leading supplier, and
from Western Europe and perhaps from the Soviet bloc. To
the extent that the Asian market is thus satisfied by Japan and
Western Europe, it will strengthen the economies of countries
in whose economic health the United States has an active
interest. Thus expanding trade with Asia may prove to be of
considerable signficance to countries in the free world to
whom trade is of much more importance than it is to the
United States. In all these circumstances, it appears that optimistic forecasts that the United States can expect to benefit
greatly in the near future from an expanding market in Asia
are not well-founded.

Opportunity for Private Investment

The third economic consideration is the possibility of a
substantial increase in the rate at which American private
investment might move into Asia. Today, there is only a
trickle of private capital flowing, and that is going largely
into special situations. To be sure, by using a Soviet rhetori-
cal technique, one could point out that the value of American
direct investments in Asia has almost doubled in the last
five years, but a more meaningful statement would be that
it grew from $307 million at the end of 1949 to $596 million at the end of 1954, an average increase of less than
$60 million per year. (The details are given in the table
on page 127.) Nor is all of this increase in the form of
a new flow of capital. Some of it consists of undistributed
earnings plowed back into the enterprise. This five-year increase in the value of direct investments in Asia of $289
million is directly comparable with an increase in American
direct investment in all countries over the same period of

$8,048 million. This comparison is, if anything, an under-statement, as neither figure includes the substantial increase in American holdings of foreign securities, a form of foreign investment that relates very little, if at all, to Asia.

The figure $60 million per year is less than the expansion program of many individual American corporations today. It may be that some of the measures proposed to stimulate private foreign investment such as investment treaties and tax concessions would lead to an increased flow of private

BOOK VALUE OF AMERICAN DIRECT INVESTMENTS
IN ASIA, 1949–1954[a]
(In millions of dollars)

Country	End of Year					
	1949	1950	1951	1952	1953	1954
India................	27	38	49	63	68	92
Indonesia............	62	58	72	74	88	66
Japan................	12	19	45	69	92	106
Philippine Republic...	132	149	163	178	188	216
Other countries[b]......	74	74	79	97	104	116
Total.............	307	338	408	481	540	596

[a] Source: U. S. Department of Commerce, "International Investments and Earnings," *Survey of Current Business* (August 1955), p. 16.
[b] Includes Burma, Cambodia, Ceylon, Hong Kong, Korea, Laos, Malaya, Netherlands, New Guinea, Pakistan, Taiwan, Thailand, and Vietnam. Data supplied directly by U. S. Department of Commerce.

capital to some areas, but the fact is that the early stages of economic development with the Asian background of nationalism do not provide a very fruitful environment in that area for long-term private American investment on any large scale.

This conclusion is not particularly surprising. Productivity is achieved by the combination of various factors of production. A successful business enterprise must be able to utilize these various elements and, in turn, must have a market. The underdeveloped country is likely to be underdeveloped in many categories from power supply to skilled workmen. The market is nonexistent or at least uncultivated. These limitations are likely to mean that the capital itself will not be as productive as it might be in some more advanced country. In addition to the operating difficulties, there are various special risks involved—civil disorder, expropriation, double taxation, conversion of local currencies into dollars, and the like—which do not add to the attractiveness of the venture. Thus capital is more likely to be invested in another advanced country, except when natural resources are paramount. In fact, American direct private investments in the small area of the United Kingdom are more than double those in all of Asia.

Not only is the prospect of investment in Asia unattractive for the private American investor, but it is also important to note that in spite of the tremendous accumulation of capital in the United States, the ever-increasing sums diverted to research are providing such rapid product and process development as to continue to maintain a high level of productivity for capital investment at home. The Marxian thesis was that a mature capitalist country would be unable to utilize its capital domestically and would have to invest abroad. To the contrary, the American picture is that, except for unusual situations, the American investor can profit more by using his capital at home than by investing it in a foreign country.

In the long run, the possibility of increased private direct investment in Asia will turn on the progress made in economic development and on the degree of hospitality demonstrated by the governments to the inflow of private capital. On both these counts, the situation seems to be improving. Nevertheless, the time seems far away when the flow can be expected to be substantial enough to warrant much consideration as an important element in the economic relations between the United States and Asia.

This completes our examination of the economic aspects of American interest in Asian development. In summary, the economic relationships involved are of some importance, although they can easily be overstressed. We have a limited interest in Asia as a source of raw materials, and Asia has a moderate economic significance to us as a market for American goods. With occasional exceptions, private capital that might go to Asia can be more productive under present circumstances if used at home. Here are marginal values that may become much more important in the future but that today cannot provide a very broad basis for American interest in Asia. They are not negligible, but neither are they imperative. Asian resources and the Asian economies are important for them, but not for us. It should be added, however, that United States policy must be a world policy and not a matter of separate considerations relating to this or that country or this or that region. There may be a sort of interlocking nature to Asian development, particularly so far as Japan is concerned. Certainly, it is likely to be of much more economic significance to Western Europe than to us, and that is a value that should not be disregarded.

Cultural Interest

Economic potentials are more easily examined than the benefits to be obtained from cultural and intellectual interchange, yet these should be an important element in our interest in any foreign area. It is interesting that in our vocabulary the adjectives indicating limited cultural development are narrow geographical terms like parochial and provincial. There is much that we can learn from and about Asia. This is recognized in the recent announcement by the deans of Columbia College that, in view of the historical and intellectual richness of the Orient, they plan to expand their general education program in humanities and contemporary civilization. "It is idle to speak seriously of a liberal . . . or a general education that does not include some understanding of Eastern civilization."[4]

One definite trend in the United States is the increase in vacation time and the shortening of the work-week. The result is to create more leisure time, time not required to be devoted to the process of making a living. This increase in free time in turn should put a greater demand on the cultural and intellectual resources available to us. We can be enriched as much or more by Japanese art and poetry as by Japanese silk and canned tunafish, by Indian science and philosophy as much as by processed jute and manganese ore. Here again is a valuable element that supports American interest in Asia. It may be fairly marginal today, but it also can grow in importance in the future.

Political Interest

Our greatest concern with Asian development, however, is neither economic nor cultural. Rather, it is our deep interest that the countries of Asia may so develop as to contribute to a peaceful world and to the wider spread of the values that we hold important. It is a tremendous area with a vast population. Life for the future would look much brighter if we could look ahead and see these countries as stable and productive societies with effective and efficient governments; with an adequate dispersion of power to prevent a dictatorship of the right or the left; with ideals of freedom and justice; and existing in an atmosphere of international good will. They would then be strong forces for peace in the world.

Unfortunately, there is a wide gap between such future hopes and the present reality. The new world will not spring full-blown out of the old. Ways of life are not changed over night and new social institutions develop their root structure

[4] *Columbia Report* (April 1956), p. 3.

in terms of decades rather than months. The generation of development—economic, social, and political—can include occasional periods of drastic change, but it is essentially a long-run process. There can be no doubt but that the Asian countries struggled hard to achieve independence in order that they might control their own future. Their freedom to do so depends in the first instance on their ability to maintain their independence, and in the second on their capacity to make sufficient progress to prevent discontent from leading to disorder and dictatorship. The first is essentially an external threat, the second is internal.

External Dangers

The main danger of external attack is from communism. There can be no doubt about the aggressive character and imperialistic purpose of communism. The United States ended the Second World War with high hopes for "one world," with the new United Nations as the preserver of the peace and the protector of nations from aggression. It soon became all too apparent that Soviet military power and Soviet expansionist policies constituted a major danger to all independent nations. The widespread postwar policy of disarmament had to be reversed and a great co-operative effort was made to build an adequate military defense in the non-Communist world as speedily as possible. This policy was extremely urgent at its inception, and its success undoubtedly explains the present reduction in the fear of outside aggression by most countries. After all, this was the purpose of the effort.

The Asian countries, in most cases, have not put much weight on the existence of an external military threat to their independence and have been more concerned with the dangers of internal subversion. They also are anti-Communist but see communism as a danger from within, building upon their misery and poverty with gaudy promises of a better future under a Communist program. The problem is complicated for them by the fact that their resources are so limited that the development of military defense is bound to be at the expense of economic development. Many of them have chosen to concentrate on the latter objective.

The important point is that the Asians may prove to be right, but if so, it will be largely the result of the American effort to build up so much military strength in the world that communism will not dare apply its military leverage in weak spots as it did in Czechoslovakia or Korea or Viet Nam.

Contrary to the Communist record, there is a clear thread in United States policy of concern for maintaining the independence of nations. The Monroe Doctrine was essentially a declaration of independence for this hemisphere, not a claim of political sovereignty by the United States nor the establishment of an economic monopoly. The Open Door notes in 1899 were aimed at preventing the possible domination of East Asia by any one power. The three wars in which the United States has engaged within my memory were all on the side of protecting one country or countries from an empire-hungry aggressor. The earlier statement of American purpose "to make the world safe for democracy" still holds good. The objective was not merely to protect American democracy. It was that each nation should be free to develop in its own way, free from the threat of attacks from outside. The recent rebuilding of American military strength is closely related to our historic position in support of independence, and as such, is serving the Asian countries as well as the rest of the free world.

Internal Dangers

It is vitally important to recognize that independence alone is not enough. Once the process of development has been initiated, it must make sufficient progress so that the gap between expectations and satisfactions will not become too wide. The future of the Asian countries can be threatened from inside by too high a measure of discontent. This can lead to dictatorship either of the right or of the left, or perhaps to a continuing state of political, economic, and social confusion with no clear motion in any direction, and poverty, disease, and ignorance left as a more or less permanent condition.

The hope of preventing such a consequence lies in the acceleration of economic development to as rapid a rate as will permit the necessary social, political, and economic changes to be absorbed without creating chaos. That the United States appears to have emphasized the external dangers is no indication of its disregard of the need for rapid internal progress. In spite of the heavy burdens of rearmament, it never stopped its programs of economic assistance, and now a real shift in emphasis is taking place. Total United States military aid to all other countries in 1955 was 31 per cent below the level of 1954, while economic aid to all countries increased by 13 per cent. In 1955 economic aid to Asian countries exceeded military aid to that area by more than 50 per cent.

Assistance in Economic Development

For most of the Asian countries, economic development means a revolution in habits of thought and action. It means drastic changes in time-honored institutions and practices. These cannot be imported, and the major effort must come from within the country. What can come from outside is limited indeed, yet it can be of strategic significance. Almost by definition, the underdeveloped countries are far behind the more advanced countries in knowledge and experience of the sort leading to increased productivity and a better utilization of resources. Therefore, technical assistance becomes of great importance. Furthermore, because of the very low level of production and income, they cannot direct much of their resources to capital formation and investment. When consumption levels are so low, no humane government can depress them still lower. Here again, capital from abroad may be significant.

The importance of foreign assistance cannot be measured in dollars and cents. Any effective program for economic development must include various propulsive actions that will start chain reactions within the country. A new road opens up a new area as a source of products and as a new market. As part of a larger economic area, its resources can now be used in more productive ways. A new power plant, an improved harbor, a fertilizer plant may all be investments with a high multiplier. Once an upward trend is established, the vicious circles that held the economy back become spirals of progress.

Aid by Trade

It is possible for the underdeveloped countries to obtain many of the goods and services they need through foreign trade. An expanding export trade would provide them with foreign currencies with which they can import raw materials as required, or capital goods for expanding productivity, or even consumer goods that may be needed to hold down the inflationary tendencies so often created by efforts at accelerating investment. Therefore, to the extent that the more advanced countries expand their purchases of Asian products, they ease the problems of the underdeveloped countries.

Exports from Asian countries (the statistics unfortunately include their exports to each other) have shown a considerable increase in recent years, as follows:[5]

[5] Based on data taken from United Nations, *Monthly Bulletin of Statistics* (February 1956), p. xvii.

	Total exports	Exports to the United States
	(In billions of dollars)	
1950	5.8	1.5
1951	8.6	1.8
1952	6.9	1.7
1953	6.2	1.4
1954	6.5	1.3
1955	7.3[6]	1.6

The bulge in 1951 and 1952 was the result of the Korean War price boom. Otherwise, the trend for total exports is strongly upward.

So far as exports to the United States are concerned, the recent trend is less clear, 1955 being only slightly above the average for the last six years. However, if one compares the conditions for Asian trade with those existing prewar, both the terms of trade and the height of tariff barriers have greatly improved so far as the United States is concerned. American import prices have risen much more than prices on American exports. This price shift as of 1955 has increased the purchasing power of goods sold in the United States in terms of goods purchased by more than $3 billion when compared with what it would have been under the price relationships of 1936-38. These are world trade figures, and it may be that the shift with respect to Asia may not be so great, but such few indicators as are available for Asian countries would seem to indicate that they have shared in the benefit.

But even though the same amount of Asian exports to the United States will buy more today than prewar, what about the actual volume of exports itself? It is evident from the figures given above that the flow of Asian products to the American market is not expanding rapidly. Except for the special case of China, this seems to be more a matter of the commodity structure than of increased barriers. In fact, if one compares today with the prewar situation, the

[6] Fourth quarter estimated.

obstacles have been greatly reduced. As a result of the rise in the price level, which has automatically decreased the significance of specific duties, and the very substantial and wide-spread reduction of duties through negotiated trade agreements, the high tariff barriers of the early thirties have been greatly reduced. To be sure, there are some few sections in the tariff schedule that have proved to be untouchable, but the general downward trend during the last two decades has been clear.

For many Asian exporters, the American tariff schedules hardly exist, as most of their export commodities are on the free list. However, their comfort is in large part offset by the painful problem of Japan, which must import to live and must export to import. Japanese exports to the United States increased to a new postwar peak of $432 million in 1955, although its imports from the United States were $200 million greater. Cries of injury or threatened injury by American competitive suppliers have grown louder and louder, and they are calling for protection by any device, even legislation by state governments. In some cases, Japan itself has set limits on exports to the United States in the hope that this will quiet the insistent demands for protection.

In spite of the shift in approach in the Reciprocal Trade Agreements Act of 1934, many people in the United States still regard the tariff problem as a domestic issue. It is still a matter not reviewed in Congress by the House Committee on Foreign Affairs or the Senate Committee on Foreign Relations but is grouped with tax and other financial problems. Nevertheless, it is a matter of foreign policy, and in this particular instance, one of special importance. Far more than most countries, the future of Japan depends on its access to foreign markets, and it is hard to see how it can build a strong economy if it is shut off not only from the market of China but also from the much more important American market.

Economic Assistance Programs

The problem of the Asian countries is more than one of being able to sell and buy abroad. It is quite apparent that even with their best efforts, they will not be able to provide for an improvement in consumption and also for an investment program that will fully meet the capital requirements of rapid economic development. In most countries of Asia, merely keeping pace with the increase in population will require a substantial investment each year.

The Communist way of meeting the problem, as demonstrated both in the Soviet Union and in China, seems to be to depress consumption and provide for investment through forced savings. This is possible in a dictatorship and a police state, but difficult in countries trying to operate under a system of popular government. Foreign capital, in the form either of loans or grants, therefore becomes crucial to the rate of their progress.

It is hardly necessary to describe the extent of the American program of economic aid, but its relation to the Asian countries is not so well known. In the immediate years after the Second World War, economic assistance involved both rationing scarce goods like tin plate and electric generators so that some part of the production might go abroad, even though they were in short supply, and also providing purchasing power to other countries. Before the Korean invasion, economic aid to all countries, net grants and net credits, had totaled nearly $25 billion. Of this amount, $4 billion went to Asia, or about 16 per cent. Half of this had gone to Japan and over one fifth to Taiwan. Since then, the proportion of American economic aid that has gone to Asia has increased steadily, from 20.2 per cent in 1952 to 44.8 per cent in 1955. (The detailed data are given in the table on page 138.) The 1955 figure of $779 million is by far the largest since the Korean War. In the program now being considered by the Congress, Asia would receive $1.1 billion

UNITED STATES GOVERNMENT NET ECONOMIC ASSISTANCE TO ASIA[a]
(In millions of dollars)

Country	1952	1953	1954	1955	Four-year Total
Afghanistan..................	—[b]	5	3	6	14
China-Taiwan...............	76	89	78	83	326
India......................	94	37	29	86	246
Indo-China..................	22	32	69	265	388
Indonesia...................	33	17	23	8	81
Japan[e]......................	64	6	42	16	128
Korea[d].....................	155	204	162	222	743
Pakistan....................	7	91	10	63	171
Philippines.................	9	24	9	12	54
Thailand....................	—[b]	5	4	13	22
Other......................	16	12	8	4	40
Total Asia...............	478	521	436	779	2,214
Total World.................	2,361	2,064	1,537	1,740	
Percentage Asia of World.....	20.2	25.2	28.4	44.8	

[a] Source: U. S. Department of Commerce, "Foreign Grants and Credits by the United States Government," *Survey of Current Business* (March 1953, April 1954, 1955, 1956.
[b] Included in "Other."
[e] Includes the Ryuku Islands.
[d] Includes aid furnished through international organizations.

of the total of $1.9 billion for nonmilitary aid, or nearly 60 per cent.

By far the leading recipient in recent years has been Korea, although it was topped in 1955 by Indo-China, both cases being less of long-run economic development programs than of postwar relief and rehabilitation. If one disregards the $487 million that went to these two areas, and undoubtedly part of it went into development projects, the balance actually advanced to all the rest of Asia in 1955 was slightly less than $300 million.

These figures undoubtedly understate the actual amounts of economic aid to Asia that should be credited to the United States. Loans and grants made by international agencies are not included, although a considerable part of their resources comes from the United States. Also, other more advanced countries that have received American assistance have sometimes acted as pipe-lines with Asian countries being the ultimate beneficiaries. Even so-called military aid may include clothing, gasoline, and other civilian-type commodities for the armed forces. It may also involve the development of installations that have both military and civilian value.

Many people have tried to estimate how much assistance would be required if we calculated it on the basis of the capacity of the underdeveloped countries to make good use of foreign aid. Most such efforts have been addressed to the needs of the underdeveloped countries as a whole and have not been restricted to Asia alone. There have been advocates of various amounts between that of the Citizens' Committee for Expanded Foreign Aid of $1.5 billion per year and Paul Hoffman's $25 billion over five years or Walter Reuther's $8 billion per year (2 per cent of the national income). Most would agree that American interest in Asian development would suggest a substantially larger figure for that area than the present one. Some of the countries have planned programs, and what is involved can be seen. The new Indian plan, for example, includes a foreign exchange deficit of about $300 million per year for the next five years. The corresponding figure for Pakistan is about $100 million.

There is, of course, a very real limit to what may be called absorptive capacity. Economic development must move forward on various fronts more or less in parallel. Capital can be valuable only in combination with raw materials, labor, and competent management. There must be power and transportation facilities. The product is valueless unless there is a market structure for it. In fact, I doubt that the 1955 amount could effectively be much more than doubled in the next three years even if we were prepared to make some risky investments. However, given the importance of the objective, I should like to feel that funds were available for every promising use in Asia for economic development. That is not the case at present.

Counterarguments

Quite contrary to the thoughts that I have been presenting, there are those who say that the United States should terminate its economic assistance programs. We can't afford them. At least, let us wait until we can use the savings from disarmament. Why not let private capital do the job? Assistance programs are likely to become permanent and that is bad. Underdeveloped countries (and soft-hearted Americans) will be wasteful, doing the wrong things and pursuing the wrong ideas like socialism or planning. And anyway, how do we know that these countries are on our side? At least, we should insist on their restricting their trade with communist countries as we do. Let us look at these various objections.

The Cost

"We can't afford it." Those who present this argument are distressed by the size of the program now before the Congress. It includes $1.9 billion for nonmilitary aid of all kinds for all areas, including relief and rehabilitation programs, aid to refugees, and assistance for economic development. Not much more than one half billion dollars appears to be earmarked for this last purpose. The total figure for all kinds of nonmilitary aid is one twentieth of the amount estimated to be spent in fiscal 1956 for the items classified as "national security" in the federal budget. It is 3 per cent of estimated net budget expenditures. It is less than one half of one per cent of our gross national product. In all but two years since the end of the Second World War, our actual economic aid programs (as distinguished from appropriations) have been considerably above this level. Our expenditures on national security rose from about $12 billion in 1948 to over $50 billion in 1953, and is currently estimated at $38.7 billion. During this same postwar period, our level of living has risen, and we have plowed back tremendous sums into new plant and equipment. Our economy has been able to meet all these requirements without strain.

We are all familiar with the problem of deciding what we can afford. It involves a choice among alternatives. Given our tremendous national income, our present levels of living, what expenditure not now being made is more important than those we are now making? If some change should be made in our pattern of expenditure, is our foreign economic assistance the marginal item that should be curtailed? My own answer clearly is, "No." Assuming that the basic purpose of economic aid is to give the underdeveloped countries the opportunity to develop into strong and stable members of the world community and that this will contribute to the maintenance of peace in the world, then the amounts involved seem small indeed, even if they were substantially increased.

It perhaps should be noted at this point that although this lecture is addressed to the American interest in Asian development, the case presented is not peculiarly American. In fact, it was pointed out that in the economic sphere, Western Europe probably has a much greater interest in Asian development than the United States. On the basic points, the importance of maintaining national independence and of developing a stronger and more stable world community, many other countries are deeply concerned. Undoubtedly many of these countries will also contribute in one way or another to Asian development, not only directly but also through their membership and contributions to various international agencies.

Comparing types of assistance, I am not sure but that the technical assistance programs are more expensive for us than the much larger commodity aid given in the form of loans and grants. The type of individual who can be valuable in a technical assistance program is valuable in any society including our own. Presumably, he must have both knowledge and experience and the ability to pass them along effectively to others. Wherever he may be, he will have a very high multiplier coefficient. Today, no country has a surplus of doctors, public health specialists, agronomists, experts on taxation, water engineers, and all the rest. The United States can more easily provide enough DDT to spray one thousand villages than it can supply the services of one public health expert for one year, although the direct costs might be ten or even a hundred to one. If the question of over-all burden of assistance programs on our society were taken at all seriously, I should start with the technical assistance programs, even though their apparent dollar cost is relatively low. The same line of reasoning would place these same programs very high on the list of forms of external assistance that can help to accelerate the processes of development. The point is that dollars are not the only measure.

There are those who would not argue that we should give up assistance programs, but who do say, "Let's hold off any appreciable expansion until we can use the savings from disarmament." There is some attractiveness to Isaiah's program for beating swords into plowshares and spears into pruning hooks. This idea in modern dress, first presented by President Truman and later reiterated by President Eisenhower, served at the time to focus attention on the burden of armaments and their diversion of resources from productive to unproductive uses. It may have rallied some added support behind the notion of disarmament, although it hardly seems as though that would be necessary. The fact is that despite the heavy burden of armaments, we can still afford economic aid up to the absorptive capacity of the

underdeveloped countries. Disarmament and economic development are both desirable in their own right, and there
is no necessary interdependence between these two objectives.

Some more sophisticated economic analysts may have the
idea that if there is disarmament, it may lead to lessened
economic activity, and the gap can then be filled by increased
assistance programs. Actually, the United States has gone
through a reduction of $12 billion in national security ex-
penditures since 1953, and the gross national product is higher
than ever. If a gap should threaten, either lower taxes or
increased programs of road and school building could easily
take up the slack. One can always hope, but the notion of
holding down our contributions of economic assistance until
an agreed program for disarmament is actually reflected in
our national estimates seems really to be nothing but a way
of delaying action.

Reliance on Private Capital

"Why not let private capital provide the aid needed?"
Surely, such direct investment would be particularly helpful
because capital would carry with it experience in how to use
it. Private capital would contribute to the flow of technology
and encourage the development of private entrepreneurship
and managerial skills.

I have already discussed the obstacles and the counter-
attractions that seem to have restricted the flow of private
capital to Asia and that make such a proposal mere wishful
thinking. In addition, it is essential to realize that the immediate capital requirements in most of Asia are largely for
social capital to provide schools, sanitation, hospitals, and the
like, and for overhead capital to provide basic economic facilities such as roads, ports, and railroads, power, and irrigation. These are essential projects, yet they frequently do not
produce immediate profits and are not attractive to foreign
direct investment.

At one time, private investors would have supplied funds

for such purposes, usually in the form of the purchase of bonds from the foreign government. However, the international capital market that used to handle this sort of foreign investment has never recovered from its collapse late in the twenties. Even European governments cannot sell securities on the American market today.

Since the Second World War, the chief device for mobilizing private capital for foreign projects has been the International Bank for Reconstruction and Development. It is a most useful instrumentality, but the fact that it obtains funds from private investors hardly brings it under the heading "private enterprise." Many of these early public investments in economic development projects make the situation much more attractive for future private investment. However, it would clearly be unrealistic to put much reliance on a significant flow of private capital at this stage of affairs.

The Endless Prospect

"It may be permanent." Permanent is too much of a word, but certainly aid for economic development has no nearby termination date like the four years of the Marshall Plan. I have already pointed out that economic development is a long, slow process, which must be considered in terms of decades rather than of years. To be sure, the most difficult phase is to get the process started. The underdeveloped country then has the greatest internal inertia, and such resources as it has are least effectively mobilized. But even if and when there is a break-through, the process of increasing productivity comes only from the combined use of all the factors of production. An advance can be made by using them more skillfully. That is where technical assistance may be helpful. Or increased production can come from having more productive factors to utilize. In most countries, the factor that is relatively most scarce is capital. Obviously, increasing the use of capital is not a one-shot operation, but a matter of continual flow and application.

If the long-range character of assistance for economic development purposes is recognized, at least two consequences flow from that fact. The first is in the matter of personnel. These operations should no longer be manned in large part by more or less temporary employees, but should involve a career service with improved recruitment, career planning, and in-service training. The second is in the matter of programing. Our present system of year-by-year appropriations greatly handicaps our effectiveness. Certainly our inventive genius should be able to find some way that would permit long-range commitments. Battleships are not built in a year, but they never lie about half-finished. For full effectiveness, we need even more power to permit mutual planning ahead than was requested by the President, even before he downgraded his proposal.

Wastefulness

"It may be used wastefully." Unfortunately, some of it will be, just as poor investments are made in the United States. We cannot expect the efficiency of modern American business, although even that can be overrated. Recent reports from Burma indicate an embarrassing surplus of cement at the ports as a result of their recent trade arrangement with the Soviet Union—a case obviously of poor programing. Underdeveloped countries are likely to be underdeveloped in public administration and in the many facilities and methods of handling that are routine in more advanced countries. We must work out methods of co-operation that will help to assure a minimum of misuse of the resources we provide. Herein lies something of a dilemma. If part of our hope is to strengthen the element of independence, this limits the degree of responsibility we should wish to take.

Certainly, we do not want to define the exact pattern to be followed in questions like the degree of governmental planning or governmental operation. In our own society, even with its strong tradition of individualism, we have called on the government more and more to set limits and rules with respect to the exercise of individual initiative. In these underdeveloped countries, with their shortage of resources and their lack of market organization, it is understandable that we find governments taking greater responsibility. This can have its dangers, for strong governments come close to dictatorships, and there is great protection in the dispersion of decisions as happens here. But conditions in Asia are different, and we must be patient and understanding of the tremendous problems that confront these countries and of the devices they select to deal with them.

East-West Trade

"They should limit their trade with Communist countries." This was an important problem in the early stages of the military build-up, when it appeared that denying certain strategic goods to the Communists would hamper and restrict their own military development. It is doubtful whether this is any longer a significant matter, as one result of the earlier policy was to force them to develop the production of the embargoed items themselves.

Now the problem is appearing in new form—not so much in the form of offers by the Communists to buy advanced technical items or strategic raw materials as proposals to trade with underdeveloped countries, and offers of technical assistance and credit to them. Certainly this is no reason for us to be willing to do less although it may mean that the demands on us will be less. Economic development can be done with Communist or free world goods, and economic development is what we hope to see.

I suppose that what we really fear is that if these countries have as much contact with Communist as with free nations, they will be more likely to move toward communism, and this may mean ultimately the loss of their independence and the weakening of the free world. In any circumstance, this is a gamble. No one can give an assurance on their future course. We can only consider the probabilities and the alternatives. These countries are not Communist today. They represent various degrees of development in democratic terms, and they are extremely sensitive in their insistence on independence. If they make economic progress, there is more than a chance that their evolution will continue to keep them out of the Communist orbit. If they receive inadequate aid from the free world and falter in their economic development, they are more likely to turn to a dictatorship of the right or the left or the military, or merely to flounder in chaos. There is no conflict between their ambitions for themselves and our hopes for them.

Ways as Well as Means

To make our assistance fully effective, we must put our best foot forward, not only in terms of programs, but also in the equally important matter of our apparent posture. There is nothing more disheartening than to travel about Asia and find out how they picture the United States. All too often, we are regarded as militaristic, delighting in rattling our sabres and playing with our rockets. We are capitalistic, and our so-called "ruling classes" are materialistic and exploitative. They say that we do not really value independence but support colonialism; our interests are strictly selfish, using foreign bases to protect our homeland and strings to obtain our *quid pro quo*. Who would not be suspicious of such a country? To us, this seems an ugly caricature, and we hardly recognize ourselves.

We sometimes seem to have been doing our best to undercut our own efforts. We have given substantial amounts of assistance, but all too often it has seemed grudging and almost unwilling. We speak with many voices too loudly. Reports of investigations are published to the world telling about the occasional failures and saying nothing of the non-spectacular gains that are made. We have seemed to lose our enthusiasm and eagerness in our immersion in the details of daily operation. We have become involved in requirements and blue-prints and engineering data. All this is not the true America. Our concern is there, the sense of mutual interest is there, but too often we have forgotten that this must be stated again and again if it is to be reflected in human relationships.

At the moment, many are saying that our foreign economic policy is a failure and that what we must have is a new model. Essentially, the problem is not with reference to what we are doing. We are still lowering trade barriers, and we have going programs of technical assistance and of economic assistance in the form of loans and grants. These are the three main ways whereby an advanced country can help in the development of another country. There are no other rabbits in the hat. The problem lies rather in the vigor of our effort and the manner in which we do it. This involves a constant concern about all our relationships with the Asian countries, not merely the economic. It involves questions of the place of the United Nations and the Colombo Plan in the general picture. And above all, it involves a much stronger and more explicit recognition on our part of our own interest in Asian development and developments in Asia.

It is not enough to have good programs or to have the very best ambassadors. Foreign policy is not merely a matter of operations abroad, but must begin at home. Too often, we regard problems with foreign implications, like tariffs or the granting of visas, for example, as domestic affairs. We need to become much more aware of the foreign effects of our domestic behavior. We need to recognize our interest in Asian development as a major element in our foreign policy, and be prepared to work at it with enthusiasm and imagination in all its many ramifications. Here is a point where human, economic, cultural, and political objectives all coincide. And happily, our basic objectives coincide with the objectives of the Asian countries. It would be a tragedy indeed if we failed somehow to establish the necessary meeting of minds and the forms of co-operation by which we might work together toward economic progress and a more peaceful world.

At times in the past, we have made tremendous sacrifices to achieve some purpose of foreign policy. To show our interest in Asian development may require us to share some of our knowledge and our productivity. We shall have to make a much greater effort to understand the Asian countries and to help them to understand us. This is a matter of imperative importance. Over the long pull, our foreign relationships rather than our domestic achievements will determine our future.

Index

Afghanistan, economic penetration by Soviet Union of, 87-88; Khrushchev-Bulganin visit to, 104-05; trade position of, 87

Africa, British institutions and, 52; changing position of peoples of, 6-8; dependence of economic growth on Middle East oil, 82-83; Islam in, 57; spread of industrialization to, 24

Agricultural commodities, United States exports to Far East of, 122-24

Akbar the Great, 52

Alisjahbana, Takdir, 99

Alliance, sources of difficulties in Western, 43-50

Alliances, unifying aim of, 38

American (See also United States), Asia and private investment, 126-29; Asia as market for goods, 122-26; British belief concerning party system, 63

American political institutions, English versus, 45-50

Arab states, use of oil as political weapon by, 83

Asia (See also Far East; Southeast Asia; individual countries), American interest in development of, 117-49; American private investment in, 126-29; as market for American goods, 122-26; as source of raw materials, 119-22; attitudes of leaders of, 105-10; changing position of peoples of, 6; co-operation with the West, 92-116; "democracy" in, 58; dependence of economic growth on Middle East oil, 82-83; diversities of, 95-97, 117-18; exports from countries of, 134-35; growth of Soviet encroachment in, 6; meaning of word as used in lecture, 117n; modernization of,

110-16; neutralism of, 13-15; political force of nationalism in, 103-04; political liberation as viewed by, 60; probable volume of East-West trade in, 87-88; similarities of, 97-98, 117-18; Soviet aid program for, 111-12; threat of Communism to, 131-32; twentieth century revolution and, 98-105; United States assistance in economic development of, 133-40; United States interest in culture of, 129-30; United States interest in politics of, 130-33; Western relations with, 7-8

"Asia for the Asians," 103

Asia Foundation, 92n

Asian-African Conference (See Bandung Conference)

Asian Development Corporation, suggested formation of, 113

Aswan dam, 87

Atomic age, Soviet-Communist claims in the, 101-02

Atomic energy, future role of, 34-35

Atoms for Peace Proposals, President Eisenhower's, 101

Australia, spread of industrialization to, 24

Bagehot, Walter, 51, 52

Balance-of-payments, positions of Far Eastern countries, 78-79

Bandung Conference, 95, 105, 108, 109, 110

Bentham, Jeremy, 51

Bentinck, Lord William, 53

Beria, Lavrenti P., 12

Berle, Jr., A. A., 84

Bretton Woods institutions, 75-77, 79-80, 88-89

British rule, India under, 52-53

Brogan, Denis W., 37-64, 97

Brown, Harrison S., 19-36

Bulganin, Nikolai A., 104

151